U.S. ARMY TRACTOR TRUCKS AND SEMITRAILERS

CASEMATE | ILLUSTRATED | SPECIAL

CASEMATE | ILLUSTRATED | SPECIAL

U.S. ARMY TRACTOR TRUCKS AND SEMITRAILERS

DIDIER ANDRES

Acknowledgements

Special thanks for their help and unwavering support to Alexandre Delbes without whom all the documentation used would not have been assembled and consulted, and Michel Roques, a long-term friend and untiring reader of texts and purveyor of great historic counsel. Special thanks to Jean-Michel Boniface for his encouragement and access to his collection of photos. Thanks to the company TM-WWII PDF Military Manuals for its availability and access to its documentation (www.tm-ww2.com).

CISS0023

Published in 2025 by
CASEMATE PUBLISHERS
1950 Lawrence Road, Havertown, PA 19083, USA
and
47 Church Street, Barnsley, S70 2AS, UK

This book is published in cooperation with, and under license from, Sophia Histoire & Collections. Originally published in French as *Les Tracteurs & Semi-Remorques de L'U.S. Army* by Didier Andres

Print Edition: ISBN 978-1-63624-590-4
Digital Edition: ISBN 978-1-63624-591-1

Translated from the French by Alan McKay
Design by Myriam Bell Design, UK
Printed and bound in the Czech Republic by FINIDR s.r.o.

CASEMATE PUBLISHERS (US)
Telephone (610) 853-9131
Fax (610) 853-9146
Email: casemate@casematepublishers.com
www.casematepublishers.com

CASEMATE PUBLISHERS (UK)
Telephone (0)1226 734350
Email: casemate@casemateuk.com
www.casemateuk.com

Title page: Autocar advert, 1944.

The publisher's authorized representative in the EU for product safety is Authorized Rep Compliance Ltd., Ground Floor, 71 Lower Baggot Street, Dublin D02 P593, Ireland.
www.arccompliance.com

Contents

Introduction
To Tow or Not to Tow?

At the end of the 1930s, two doctrines opposed each other in the United States Army, which had indeed begun restructuring in a far-reaching way.

As far as rolling stock was concerned, this struggle for influence concerned all vehicle types, but initially, the technical vehicles were the main concern. It was only while these were developing that reflection widened to include all means of transport.

The proponents of the trailer, or the semitrailer, recommended that the mechanical part (the truck tractor) be separated physically from the technical part (the trailer) which carried the special equipment. This view was justified by practical considerations: if the traditional truck broke down, not only was the mechanical part immobilized but the technical part, too. The same thing would happen too when the technical part, once in use, had to go into a workshop: the mechanical part was immobilized. Whichever way one looked at it, one part was always immobilized.

For the supporters of smaller, inseparable ensembles, strategic thoughts prevailed. In the case of military operations, mechanical and technical outfits consisting of a single vehicle were easier to move around, saving time if there was a withdrawal—as the technical part did not have

A semitrailer is a road trailer for transporting merchandise whose characteristic was to rest on one or several axles at the rear and on the tractor at the front, by means of a platform called the fifth wheel, so that the tractor took a large part of the weight of the trailer and its load.

A semitrailer—like this Map Reproduction Semitrailer—uncoupled from its tractor became a dead weight for a unit which had to move quickly. This was the theory of detractors of the truck tractors who recommended single monobloc truck outfits. (Private Collection)

to be hitched up—and, above all, the mechanical components were on hand for all the technical components.

Each of the two doctrines was persuasive. However, during the interwar period, the trailers had the edge, and the solution adopted by all the parts of the army at the beginning of the 1940s was a blend of the two different trends. The technical truck bodies were both mounted on a truck chassis and on trailers, the two types of vehicles being separated theoretically by the front line and the immediate rear area. Basically, the front was ideally served only by complete trucks; the rest of the theater of operations, being normally safer and therefore more accessible, was covered by tractors and semitrailers. Lots of truck tractors were created because of this; all the payload categories that characterized American military cartage were included. The truck tractors were also divided into two large categories: the 4x2 or 6x4 road tractors; and the full 4x4 or 6x6-wheel-drive multipurpose tractors. Civilian-produced vehicles initially

1937/38 Model Chevrolet and semitrailer. (U.S. Signal Corps)

Despite the momentum in bringing equipment up to date, old models of light truck trailers remained in service, like here at Port Reno in October 1941. (U.S. Army SC-131777)

All these semitrailers in use at the beginning of the 1940s were very cramped and the Army's rapid expansion could not be carried out. A whole cartage had to be created, both for the tractors and the trailers. (U.S. Army SC-125583)

formed this fleet of semitrailer tractors. They were small-sized vehicles of the 4x2 1½-ton type. The traditional manufacturers like Dodge, Chevrolet or Ford were the first to benefit from this new market. The semitrailers all basically resembled each other and were of the 2½-ton category with different types of doors, windows, and interior fixtures and fittings.

Initially, this category was built up by adopting the 4x4 tractors and shifting from the 1½-ton to the 2½-ton category. But above all, these new trucks were at first intended for specialized roles, like the Signal Corps with the Autocar U-5044, the Cavalry with the GMC AFKX-502, or again the U.S. Army Air Forces with the Autocar U-4144 and U-4144-T. For instance, transporting horses could be done by stake-and-platform-type semitrailers or by trucks alone of the GMC AFKX-353 17-foot type. It was, however, in the Corps of Engineers that this harmonization worsened. Thus, the special topography, photography, workshops, sewage, tanker semitrailers, all had their "reduced" version based on a Diamond T or GMC truck.

From a few truck tractors with a limited capacity in 1940, dozens of models in all weight and mechanical categories had been allocated by 1945. Great families of trucks like the Autocars, the Federals, and the International Harvesters appeared but often there were also successful in-the-field adaptations.

1 1½-Ton Truck Tractor Category

This category of semitrailer tractors was the transition between peace and the war that was beginning to stir in different parts of the world.

America was not ready to go to war again; it had gone to sleep after November 1918 and the specter of the trenches in France made it withdraw into itself. When it became necessary to renew the truck tractors in service, the Quartermaster Corps and the Ordnance Department turned at first to the range of civilian vehicles that were easily adaptable to their needs. The first firm to be consulted—Chevrolet—delivered the first new 1½-ton 4x2 truck tractors in 1940. It was soon followed by Ford and Dodge supplying the 2,121 examples. It was only in 1941 that the 4x4 version of these little semitrailer tractors came out, of which 2,943 examples were delivered by Chevrolet.

1½-Ton 4x2 Chevrolet

Overall, 891 vehicles of this type were delivered, of which 270 were directed at once to the Defense Aid program. Supplies were spread out over three years: 182 in 1940, 223 in 1941, and the last 486 in 1942.

They were accepted in 10 orders and three appellations, the first 61 being WAs in the builder's nomenclature (registration numbers USA-W-410783 to USA-W-410785, USA-W-317821 to USA-W-317877 and USA-W-317879), 216 were accepted with the reference G-4103-MR (USA-W-365312 to USA-W-365527) and 323 with the reference G-4103 (USA-W328443 to USA-W-328550,

These small tractors came directly from the civilian product ranges and still had some of the chrome work. This Dodge T-118 has not yet been given its military registration number; it is towing an early 3-ton semitrailer van. (U.S. Army Signal Corps)

Having just arrived at the Holabird Quartermaster Depot in Baltimore, this Chevrolet is waiting for its platform before going through its series of tests. (U.S. Army SC-125952)

USA-W-331895 to USA-W-339403, and USA-W-339337 to USA-W-339403); 21 did not receive any registration numbers at all because they were sent to a government agency.

The ensemble had its two differentials with a wheelbase of 134.5 inches (341.63 cm); it was 79.5 inches (201.93 cm) high, 82.5 inches (209.55 cm) wide, and 198.5 inches (504.19 cm) long. It weighed 4,165 lb (1,892 kg) and could tow semitrailers weighing at most 12,000 lb (5,448 kg) but could not carry more than 4,670 lb (2,120 kg) on its fifth wheel. The vehicle's braking system was hydraulic and that of the towed trailers was electric.

With 7.00x20 8-ply tires, the Chevrolet was powered by a BG-1001 gasoline engine made up of a single block comprising six piston chambers.

Although these are 4x2 vehicles, they have been incorporated into the motorized units, and these two examples of Chevrolets are standing alongside new Ford GP Jeeps and GMC CCKWXs. (U.S. Army Signal Corps)

It was water cooled, with a capacity of 235.5 cubic inches (3,860 cc), rated at 83.5 bhp at 3,000 rpm. The transfer of the engine's power was through a simple dry-disk clutch, and a gearbox with four forward and one reverse gears. With these mechanics and with an 18-gallon (68.13-liter) fuel tank, all models had a range of some 108 miles (174 km), a consumption rate of some 6 mpg. This consumption average varied depending on the type of road, the traveling conditions, and whether it was towing.

1½-Ton 4x2 Dodge

A single order was made for 116 Dodges referenced T-118 by the manufacturer; all were delivered in 1941 and registered in a single series (USA-W-353494 to USA-W-353609). This relatively small number of vehicles was because the manufacturer was engaged in the plentiful WC ½-ton program and it could not produce more truck tractor orders.

The ensemble had two differentials with a wheelbase of 134.3 inches (341.15 cm); the tractor was 80 inches (203.2 cm) high, 80.2 inches (203.67 cm) wide, and 196 inches (497.84 cm) long. It weighed 4,490 lb (2,039 kg) and could tow semitrailers weighing at most 12,000 lb (5,448 kg) but could not take more than 4,670 lb (2,120 kg) on its fifth wheel. The vehicle's braking system was hydraulic and that of the towed trailers was electric. With 7.00x20 8-ply tires, the Dodge was powered by a BG-1001 gasoline engine made up of a single block comprising six piston chambers. It was water cooled, with a capacity of 236.6 cubic inches (3,878 cc), rated at 104 bhp at 3,000 rpm. The transfer of the engine's power was through a simple dry-disk clutch, with four forward and one reverse gears. With these mechanics and an 18-gallon (68.13-liter) fuel tank, all models had a range of some 126 miles (203 km), a consumption rate of some 7 mpg. This consumption average varied depending on the type of road, the travelling conditions, and whether it was towing.

1½-Ton 4x2 Ford

With 1,115 examples distributed between three orders, Ford was the first 1½-ton 4x2 truck supplier in terms of numbers and duration with 263 examples in 1941, 537 in 1942, 54 in 1943, and 260 in 1944. The first series concerned 300 Ford 2GTs (USA-W-364714 to USA-W-365013), the second series 500 2G8Ts

Top: Manufacturer Type G-4103-YP for this third-generation Chevrolet tractor with the registration number USA-W-339398. (TM 10-1475)

Middle: Be it Dodge, Chevrolet or, as here, Ford, the three vehicles had the same usual features with the driving cabin behind the engine compartment. (G-658)

Bottom: Registration number USA-W-328765 for this Chevrolet Truck Tractor Model YP-G-4112-YK that has not been given its fifth wheel yet. (U.S. Army SC-123888)

Coming also from the first series of the YP-G-4112-YKs, this one was registered as USA-W-328766), or Chevrolet Truck Tractor No. 6. (U.S. Army Signal Corps)

(USA-W-368869 to USA-W-369368), and the last 314 being 2G8TAs (USA-328886 to USA-353609 and USA-3397552 to USA-3397811).

The ensemble had two differentials with a wheelbase of 141 inches (358.14 cm); the tractor was 83.5 inches (212.09 cm) high, 86 inches (218.44 cm) wide and 202 inches (513.08 cm) long. It weighed 5,800 lb (2,633 kg) and could tow semitrailers weighing at most 12,000 lb (5,448 kg) but could not carry more than 4,300 lb (1,952 kg) on its fifth wheel. The vehicle's braking system was hydraulic and that of the towed trailers was electric.

With 7.50x20 8-ply tires, the truck was powered by a Model G8 gasoline engine of the brand, consisting of a single block comprising six piston chambers. It was water cooled, with a capacity of 225.78 cubic inches (3,701 cc), rated at 90.7 bhp at 3,400 rpm. The transfer of the engine's power was through a simple dry-disk clutch, with a four forward and one reverse gears. With these mechanics and a 19-gallon (71.92-liter) fuel tank, all models had a range of some 114 miles (183 km) and its consumption rate was some 6 mpg.

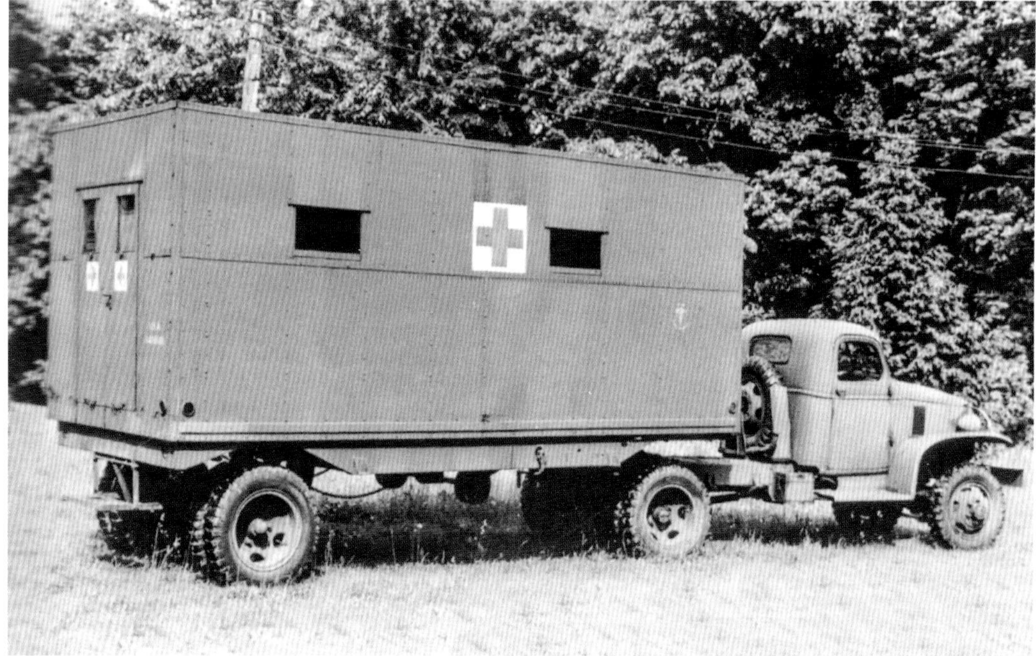

Despite the standardization, several private productions saw the light of day like this 2½-ton Surgical Semitrailer for the Medical Department seven examples of which were built, and trailers for command posts. 1940 was the beginning of a vast program of allocations. (U.S. Army ORD-3664)

1½-Ton 4x4 Chevrolet

3,530 examples of the military all-wheel drive version were ordered but only 2,943 were delivered; there were seven orders for 8 units delivered in 1940, 137 in 1941, 1,379 in 1942, 1,226 in 1943 and 193 in 1944. Depending on the production, the manufacturer's type was YP-G-4112-YK for the first eight, ZP-G-4165-ZK for the next 89 and G-7113-NK for the rest.

The ensemble had two differentials with a wheelbase was 145 inches (368.3 cm), the tractor was 87 inches (220.98 cm) high, 85.75 inches (217.8 cm) wide, and 206 inches (523.24 cm) long. It weighed 6,140 lb (2,788 kg) and could tow semitrailers weighing at most 12,000 lb (5,448 kg) but could not take more than 4,850 lb (2,202 kg) on its fifth wheel. The vehicle's braking system was identical to the other vehicles in this chapter.

With 7.00x20 8-ply tires, the Chevrolet 4x4 was powered by a Chevrolet gasoline engine, made up of a single block comprising six piston chambers. It was water cooled, with a capacity of 235.5 cubic inches (3,860 cc), rated at 93 bhp at 3,100 rpm. The transfer of the engine's power was through a simple dry-disk clutch, with four forward and one reverse gears, and a two-stage transfer box. With these mechanics and a 30-gallon (113.55-liter) fuel tank, all models had a range of some 270 miles (435 km), a consumption rate of some 9 mpg. This average varied, depending on the type of road, the travelling conditions, and whether it was towing.

Semitrailers

Like all the 1½-ton 4x4 Chevrolets, the semitrailers adapted to the truck tractors were extensively covered in *U.S. Army Chevrolet Trucks in World War II* (2020). Although at first these 4x2 truck versions were designed for towing prewar outfits, when the 4x4s appeared, they were accompanied by two new models, the 3½-ton Stake and Platform (S&P) Semitrailer, of which 1,818 examples were delivered to the Army, plus 141 others intended for Defense Aid, and the 3- or 3½-ton Semitrailer Van, of which 2,259 units were delivered.

Above: 3½-ton Stake and Platform (S&P) Semitrailer. Its registration number (USA-W-043304) meant it was made by Winter Weiss Co. These semitrailers with a single axle and 7.50x20 8-ply twin tires had a wheelbase of 148 inches (375.92 cm) for a total length of 201 inches (510.54 cm), a width of 84 inches (213.36 cm), and a height of 89 inches (226.02 cm). With an empty weight of 4,953 (2,247 kg) they could take a weight of 7,006 lb (3,178 kg). The spread of the weight was 4784 lb (2,170 kg) on the tractor's fifth wheel, and 7,176 lb (3,255 kg) on the axle, or a weight distribution ration of 40% and 60%. There were 1,818 examples delivered. (U.S. Army SC-127219)

Below: Semitrailer Van 3- or 3½-ton. These semis with a single axle and 7.50x20 8-ply twin tires with a 162-inch (411.48-cm) wheelbase for a total length of 216 inches (548.64 cm), a width of 87.74 inches (222.88 cm), and a height of 128.75 inches (327.02 cm). With an empty weight of 4,927 (2,235 kg) they could take a weight of 6,003 lb (2,723 kg). The spread of the weight was 4,515 lb (2,048 kg) on the tractor's fifth wheel, and 7,363 lb (3,340 kg) on the axle, or a weight distribution ration of 38% and 62%. There were 2,259 examples delivered. (U.S. Army SC-127223)

2 2½-Ton Truck Tractor Category

GMC AFKX-502

A vehicle was rarely bought for a single function, but this was the case of the GMC AFKX-502, a 4x4 tractor classified in the 2½-ton category, of which only 81 examples were ordered and delivered.

At the beginning of the 1940s, when it was reformed and mechanized, the Army equipped its cavalry units with vehicles and special trailers for moving men and horses around over long distances.

There were 81 truck tractors ordered under the contract W-398-QM-7542 with registration numbers taken in a series ranging from USA-W-412792 to USA-W-412872. There was no question of creating a completely new truck; it was a question of using an existing commercial model and adapting it slightly, so it conformed to Army standards. General Motors Truck & Coach (GMC) was given this order and modified a civilian truck by, for example, giving it a front engine differential. The AFKX-502s were all delivered in 1940 and were designed for towing the 6-ton Combination Animal & Cargo Semitrailers with a carrying capacity of eight horses, together with their riders as well as all the necessary equipment.

The Shape

The GMC AFKX-502 was a cab-over-engine (COE)-type tractor with a technical part on a fifth wheel at the rear. Made on a chassis with two main longerons and six intermediary crossmembers, this ensemble had two differentials with a 136-

The ranges of civilian vehicles were used as a base for the GMC AFKX-502. Militarizing them changed these road trucks into 4x4 vehicles and gave them a design with purer and more aerodynamic lines. (Private Collection)

Right: With its registration number USA-W-412792, this example of an AFKX-502 was the first of 81 examples, ordered with the contract W-398-QM-7542. (U.S. Army SC-124553)

Below: February 2, 1941, a column of AQFKX-502s leaving Fort Oglethorpe with its shipment of men and horses. The only special modification made to the trucks is the position of the little marker lights on the headlight casings. (ACME 591616)

Right: Despite its offroad capability made possible by its four-wheel drive, the AFKX-502 was not intended as a front-line vehicle. Its job was to bring the cavalry units closer to the front to spare the mounts. (U.S. Army SC-123044)

inch (345.44-cm) wheelbase. Built only with a closed-in metal cab, the tractor was 105 inches high (266.7 cm), 95 inches (233.68 cm) wide, and 202 inches (513.08 cm) long. Its only gasoline tank was located on the left-hand side of the chassis. On the right-hand side, the empty space on the longeron was occupied by a large toolbox; both sides had a protective fairing. The two spare wheels were located vertically on the back of the cabin.

With a net weight of 8,565 lb (3,888 kg), the KR-11 could tow semitrailers with a maximum weight of 20,000 lb (9,080 kg) but with not more than 9,350 lb (4,245 kg) on the tractor's fifth wheel. The vehicle's braking system—for the trailer too—was of the compressed-air type, a Westinghouse Automotive Air Brake System. The system was fed by a belt-driven two-cylinder compressor from the engine power takeoff, the air produced being stocked in two cylindrical tanks mounted between the longerons of the chassis.

Quick-fit connectors for the trailer brakes were located at the back of the cabin, between the cradles supporting the spare wheels.

The Mechanics

Using 10.00x20 8-ply tires, the GMC AFKX-502 rested on a WIS-F-552-TW-X Wisconsin front differential and on a TD-5003-TW- X-1 Timken-Detroit rear differential, both being of the double reduction type. The vehicle was powered by a single block 6-cylinder GM Model 308 gasoline engine. The engine with culverted valves had a capacity of 302 cubic inches (4,949.78 cc), rated at 122 bhp at 2,600 rpm. It was water cooled by a radiator made up of vaned tubes and a water pump located on the front of the engine block, ventilation being by means of a five-bladed fan to increase the cooling of its 25 quarts (23.65 liters) which made up the cooling circuit.

Top: A perfect example of the contrast between specific tractors and special trucks with the same role: in the foreground a Stock Rack ACKWX-353 designed for transporting four men and four horses; in the background AFKX-502 and semitrailers. (U.S. Army Signal Corps)

Middle: A Combination Animal & Cargo Semitrailer loaded and coupled up; a convoy is about to set off. (U.S. Army SC-115279)

Bottom: Large 1941 summer maneuvers in Louisiana; the HQ Troop of the 1st Cavalry Division unloads its trailers. At the time, unit markings were painted on the vehicle accesses. (U.S. Army Signal Corps)

Top left: Holabird Quartermaster Depot in Baltimore, March 18, 1941. Recently delivered, this 6-ton Combination Animal & Cargo Semitrailer was part of the first lot, consisting of 81 examples. (U.S. Army SC-127223)

Top right: A canvas tarp was available. It covered the whole trailer while enabling the accesses located on its right-hand side to be reached. (U.S. Army Signal Corps)

Above: The animals were loaded/unloaded using the whole ramp, the three parts being let down to guarantee optimum stability under the animals' hooves. (U.S. Army Signal Corps)

Right: Used also for troop transport, the Combination Animal & Cargo Semitrailer was certainly the most multipurposed trailer in the Army. Only a third of the ramp was used for such operations. 2nd Cavalry Division, Fort Clark, Texas, February 26, 1943. (U.S. Army SC-171265)

Above: A gathering of the column's various elements, where the troopers are in the compartment with an all-round view reserved for them. (ACME 591617)

Transferring the engine drive through the single dry-disk W.C. Lippe clutch was by means of a Clark 204VO-254 gearbox with five forward and one reverse gears, and a Wisconsin WIS-T-2-B-4-3 two-stage transfer box which also engaged the front differential, transforming the 4x2 into a 4x4.

This mechanical system, a Stromberg carburetor, an AC pump, and a 45-gallon (170.33-liter) fuel tank, gave the GMC AFKX-502 a range of between 143¾ and 187½ miles, a consumption rate of between 3.20 and 4.16 mpg, this consumption varying with the type of road, the running conditions, and the

Right: Preparations before leaving on maneuvers with the horses being embarked and the tarp being unfolded. (ACME 591615)

configuration—whether towing or not. The high consumption rate was enough for the short missions and distances for which they were intended.

The whole electrical system worked on 6 volts with positive earth from two 6-volt batteries set up in parallel, except for starting the engine which used a 12-volt starter. It was thanks to the electrical circuit of the ignition contactor, alone fed by the two batteries in series via an electromagnetic contactor, that the difference was possible. Most of the electrical parts were made by Delco-Remy.

Making a semitrailer specific to the AFKX-502 was closely linked to that of its tractor. Like it, the first 81 vehicles were delivered in 1940 with the registration numbers USA-W-04272 to USA-W-04327 for the first 56, and USA-W-04579 to USA-W-04603 for the remaining 25. In 1942, 1,107 new examples made up the fleet, without being allocated to the AFKX-502s, but rather to the new 4/5-ton 4x4 generation of truck tractors.

Four other series of registration numbers were then allocated: USA-W-018541 to USA-W-019220, USA-X-039187 to USA-W-039223, USA-W-039409 to USA-W-039459, and USA-W058788 to USA-W-059126.

Two companies shared the order, the Highway Trailer Co. (the SKD-1815) with 339 units and the Trailer Co. of America (Model TD-32-G) for the next 849. These single-axle cargo semitrailers with 9.00x20 10-ply twin tires had a 225-inch (571.98-cm) wheelbase (from the axle to the coupling point) for a total length of 289¼ inches (734.7 cm), a width of 96 inches (243.84 cm), and a height of 126 inches (320.04 cm). With an empty weight of 8,827 lb (4,004 kg), they could take a weight of 12,010 lb (5448 kg). With a maximum payload, the spread of the weight was 8,126 lb (3,686 kg) on the tractor's fifth wheel and 12,711 lb (5,766 kg) on the axle, or a distribution ratio of 39% and 61%.

The GMC AFKX 502s were very quickly considered obsolete and it was not the 81 examples that enabled the 1,188 6-ton Combination Animal & Cargo Semitrailers bought by the Army to be moved. More modern tractors carried out these missions, especially the 4x4 4/5-ton or the 4x2 5-ton Truck Tractors. (U.S. Army Signal Corps)

Studebaker US6 6x4 & 6x6

The Studebaker US6 (G630) was a series of 2½-ton 6x6 and 5-ton 6x4 trucks. The basic cargo version was designed to transport a 2½-ton (5,000-lb; 2,300-kg) cargo load over any type of terrain in any weather.

There were 8,640 semitrailers of the 6x4 version in the 2½-ton category ordered from the Studebaker Corporation. This class of trucks started at the same time as a great challenge at the opening of the war: how to supply the Allies quickly, over long distances using existing technology. As the program of the 2½-ton 6x6 trucks had already started, all that was needed was for a road vehicle with a truck tractor's capacities to be created. As the GMC company had already been overwhelmed by orders since 1941, Studebaker inherited the project and delivered 8,640 vehicles. The Army only kept 2,346 examples for itself, the remaining 6,294 were supplied in the context of the Defense Aid and Lend-Lease programs, or 4,466 to the United Kingdom and 1,828 to Russia. A new trailer was also designed, the 7-ton Cargo Semitrailer. 7,752 were built and were supplied to England and the Red Army in the same proportions, leaving only 1,458 units for the U.S. Army.

The Shape

These Studebaker US6s were quite traditional trailer tractors, with the driving cabin behind the engine compartment and the technical part on the fifth wheel at the rear. Made on a chassis with two main longerons with five intermediary crossmembers, this outfit had three differentials with a 148-inch (375.92-cm) wheelbase. Built only with a closed metal cabin, the tractor was 88 inches (223.52 cm) high, 86.75 inches (220.35 cm) wide, and 220 inches (558.8 cm) long.

Weighing 8,140 lb (3,696 kg) net, the US6 6x4 U6 could tow semitrailers weighing at most 21,510 lb (9,766 kg) on the road but could not carry more than 9,520 lb (4,322 kg) on the tractor's fifth

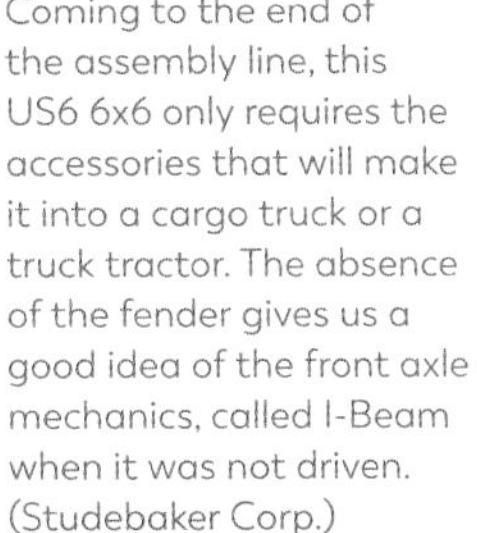

Coming to the end of the assembly line, this US6 6x6 only requires the accessories that will make it into a cargo truck or a truck tractor. The absence of the fender gives us a good idea of the front axle mechanics, called I-Beam when it was not driven. (Studebaker Corp.)

Used for moving around, short of a semitrailer of the Low Bed 45,000-lb type, this US6 6x4 is at the extreme limit of its capacities. The braking systems being incompatible, there was no connection between the tractor and the trailer. The indications on the container being transported state that it contains a Diamond T 968. (U.S. Army PGO-559)

wheel. The braking system of the vehicle was of the hydraulic-vacuum type, the same for the trailer.

The Mechanics

Using 7.50x20 8-ply tires, the Studebaker lay on a free-running front differential of the I-Beam type, the Clark F-550, and on two Timken-Detroit NX-5s, references 53661 and 53662. The vehicle was powered by a Hercules JXD gasoline engine consisting of a single engine block with one lateral cylinder head of the type with six pistons. It had a capacity of 320 cubic inches (5,245 cc), and was rated at 87 bhp at 2,400 rpm; it was water cooled by a radiator made of finned tubes and had a water pump located on the front of the engine block, ventilation being by means of a five-blade fan to increase the cooling of the 21 quarts (19.87 liters) comprising the cooling circuit.

Transferring the engine power was with a W.C. Lippe single dry-disk clutch, through a Warner Gera Model T93 gearbox with five forward and one reverse gears, and a T-70-5 two-stage Timken-Detroit transfer box. With this mechanical system, a Carter carburetor, an AC pump, and a 40-gallon (151.40-liter) gasoline tank giving it a range of some 250 miles (402 km) by itself and 180 miles (290 km) coupled up with a full payload; it had an average gasoline consumption of between 6¼ mpg and 4½ mpg, depending on the type of road surface, the driving conditions, and whether it was towing. All the electrics worked on 6 volts, from a single battery, with most of the electrical systems made by Auto-lite.

Normandy, August 7, 1944, two Studebaker US6 6x4 U6s in British colors entering the depot of the U.S. 607th Ordnance Ammunition Company; they are towing 7-ton Cargo Semitrailers made of wood. (U.S. Army SC-275437)

Designed one for the other, the trailer and the tractor formed a coherent, well-proportioned outfit. (U.S. Army Signal Corps)

Studebaker US6 6x4 U6 Production			
Quantity	Orders	Registration Numbers	Comments
2,050	W-271-ORD-2562-DA-188	Without registration number	All delivered in 1942
44	W-271-ORD-2681	4370797 to 4370840	All delivered in 1942
1,968	W-271-ORD-2581	4448386 to 4449265	All delivered in 1943 (nine of which modified into Dump Truck)
1,874	W-271-ORD-3854	4551667 to 4553550	900 delivered in 1943 and 974 in 1944
2,016	ORD-11-022-277	4629923 to 4631938	1,283 delivered in 1944 and 733 in 1945
270		4652669 to 4652938	All delivered in 1945
408		4839019 to 4839426	All delivered in 1945
10	ORD-11-022-277	4618812 to 4618821	All delivered in 1945

7-Ton (10-Ton Gross) Cargo Semitrailer

This semitrailer was built with either a wooden or a metal superstructure. 7,752 examples were built by 12 different manufacturers, the first 2,050 units being received in 1942, the rest being as follows: 2,086 in 1943, 3,000 in 1944, and the last 616 in 1945. As its tractor did not have any system for producing compressed air, the braking system on the trailer also worked with the hydraulic-vacuum system. The compact form of this semitrailer and the fact that it was towed by a vehicle whose fifth wheel was positioned above a double differential meant the intermediary supporting gantry had to be stepped back otherwise there was a risk of it upending forward.

One of the main routes the Western allies used to supply the USSR was by the south through the desert wastes of Iran. Called the "Persian Corridor," the route was used by innumerable convoys. In March 1943, the War Office sent the photographer Nick Parrino with a convoy, almost exclusively made up of Studebaker US6 6x4 U6s. (War Office 28459E)

Left: All along the route, each resupply point was carefully positioned, like this British Petroleum gas station. Two odd facts: all the tractors have only one headlight, the right-hand one having been removed, and the registration numbers are not preceded by the letters USA because these vehicles are on their way to be delivered to the Red Army. (War Office 28311E)

Below: All the trailers in this convoy are all-metal 7-ton Cargo Semitrailers. (War Office 28334E)

7-Ton Cargo Semitrailer Manufacturers and Registration Numbers

Wooden Superstructure Version	
Carter	0566918-0567267 / 0634602-063472 / 0936153-0936202
Edwards	0560657-0560717 / 0485390-0485469 / 0634318-0634601/ 0717977-0718558 / 0818172-0818671 / 0937433-0937464
Fruehauf	0717190-0717641
Gramm	0378086-0378685 / 0560585-0560656 / 0634086-0634241
Hyde	0560368-0560584 / 0633946-0634016 / 0684418-0684565
Nabor	0319471-0320070 / 0634722-0634929
Pointer	0566718-0566917 / 0634017-0634085
Reliance	0748829-0748956
The other 430 trailers of this type had no registration number and were delivered in the context of the Defense Aid program.	

Metal Superstructure Version	
Eidall	0934000-0934031
Miller	0936793-0936794
The other 1,620 trailers of this type had no registration numbers and were delivered in the context of the Defense Aid program.	

Stake & Platform (S&P) Version	
Edwards	0320071-0320558 / 0377886-0378085

To counteract this risk, an extra foldable leg was placed on either side of the front section. On the wooden structures, the folded-up position was vertical whereas on the steel version, it was horizontal. These 7-ton Cargo Semitrailers were also special in that they were the only ones to have a rear tailgate which opened downward, like a simple cargo truck.

The metal version was made of stamped panels which guaranteed the rigidity of the superstructure. (War Office 28465E)

The terrible conditions during the convoys and then during operations in Russia meant that the metal closed-in cabin was never replaced on the production lines in the United States. (U.S. Army SC-170223)

Another particularity of all this production: there were also 688 wooden vehicles whose superstructure was not fixed and in one piece; they were the 7-ton Stake and Platforms (S&P) Semitrailers with removable sides to change the semitrailer into a platform for unimpeded loading on three sides.

Like the AFKX-502 coupling, this trailer was produced in the same way as the US6 6x4 U6. Eight of the 12 companies delivered the 6,098 wooden examples; the 1,654 metal ones were made by the four others. 23 series of registration numbers were allocated to 5,702 of the 7,752 7-ton Cargo Semitrailers, the 2,050 trailers with no registration numbers being part of the Defense Aid program. These cargo semitrailers with a single axle and twin 7.50x20 10-ply tires had a 144-inch (367.66-cm) wheelbase (from the axle to the coupling point); it was 197 inches (500.38 cm) long, 91.5 inches (232.41 cm) wide, and 95 inches (241.3 cm) high. With an empty weight of 5,405 lb (2,452 kg), they could take a weight of 14,012 lb (6,356 kg). The distribution of the weight allowed 7,806 lb (3,541 kg) to rest on the truck's fifth wheel and 11,812 lb (5,358 kg) on its axle, or a distribution ratio of 40% and 60%.

The 7-ton Cargo Semitrailer with a wooden superstructure in its parked position, with its two extra support legs. The rear side had all the characteristics of a truck with its tailgate and even a safety harness. (SNL G-544)

Autocar U-4044, U-4144T, & U-5044

These two models were the modern basis used to highlight the features of military truck tractors in the 4/5-ton and 5/6-ton categories, designed a year later.

U-4044

Coming directly from the Autocar Company's civilian experience, this was a prompt response to the fresh needs of the U.S. Army and the U.S. Army Air Forces. These purchases were made so quickly that initially, no technical manual was published, just a "militarized" compilation of the civilian manual called *Care and Operation*.

The first supplies concerned the 99 U-4044, 4x4 2½-ton Truck Tractors ordered and delivered in 1940 (registration numbers USA-W-413527 to USA-W-413613 and USA-W-413716 to USA-W-413727) under the contract W-398-OM-7902, and in 1941 for 449 others under the contract W-398-QM-8534 (USA-W-417599, USA-W-428106 to USA-W-428338 and USA-W-428374 to USA-W-428588), a total of 548 examples.

The Autocar U-4044s were semitrailer tractors of the COE type and the technical part with a fifth wheel at the rear. Made on a chassis with two main longerons and five intermediate crossmembers, this outfit had two differentials with a 131-inch (332.74-cm) wheelbase. Built only with a closed metal cabin, the tractor was 103.5 inches (262.89 cm) high, 92.5 inches (234.95 cm) wide, and 201 inches (510.54 cm) long.

Left: The first Autocar tractor manuals delivered to the Army were civilian manuals with a sticker. (Private Collection)

Below: The Autocar firm had good experience of semitrailer tractors and it was easy for it to respond to the Army's requirements. Its U-30 was a good example. (Autocar Co.)

Weighing 10,200 lb (4,631 kg) net, the U-4044 could tow semitrailers weighing at most 20,000 lb (9,080 kg) on the road, but could only carry 5,000 lb (2,070 kg) on the tractor's fifth wheel. The braking system of the vehicle functioned both on the trailers and the haulage and was of the Westinghouse Automotive Air Brake System hydraulic-vacuum type. It was fed by a bicylinder compressor driven directly by the engine; the air produced was stocked in a cylindrical tank. Quick-fit fixtures for the trailer's brakes were located directly behind the cabin.

Using 9.00x20 10-ply tires, the U-4044 lay on two Timken-Detroit differentials, an F-551-TW for the front and an R-5002-TW for the rear, both being of the double reduction type. The vehicle was powered by a Hercules JXD gasoline engine which was made up of a single engine block housing six pistons. Having a capacity of 320 cubic inches (5,245 cc), it was rated at 110 bhp at 2,500 rpm; it was water cooled from a radiator made with finned tubes and a water pump located on the front of the engine block, ventilation being by means of a five-blade fan to increase the cooling of the 23 quarts (21.76 liters) making up the cooling circuit.

Above and center: USA-W-413527 was the first registration number allocated to the U-4044 model. This has been coupled to an F2 2,000-gallon, 6-ton Fuel Servicing Semitrailer for aircraft. The outfit did a series of tests to validate the ensemble's behavior on uneven terrain. (Autocar Co.)

Right: This, the 40th U-4044, if we go by the registration number list, bears the splendid yellow regulation livery for vehicles operating on military aerodromes. (Autocar Co.)

Above: The U.S. Army Air Corps ordered some tractors for the runways, and they often proved better than the theoretical performances they were supposed to have. Here are two F2 Semitrailers, the second of which is resting on a dolly. (U.S. Army Signal Corps)

Transferring the engine power was through a W.C. Lippe single dry-disk clutch, with a Clark Model 200-VO gearbox with five forward and one reverse gears, and a T-2-B7-4 two-stage Timken-Detroit transfer box to engage the front differential, transforming the 4x2 into a 4x4. With this mechanical system, a Stromberg carburetor, an AC pump, and a 40-gallon (151.40-liter) gasoline tank gave it a range of some 430 miles (690 km) by itself and 160 miles (260 km) coupled to a full payload, or an average gasoline consumption of between 4 mpg and 10¾ mpg, depending on the type of road surface, the driving conditions, and whether it was towing.

All the electrics worked on 6 volts, from a single 6-volt battery, most of the electrical systems being made by Delco-Remy.

U-4144T

The orders were increased and rapidly sent to the builder, for 2½-ton 4x4 Tractors. It was for 271 U-4144-Ts, under the contract W-398-QM-9433 (USA-W-460325 to USA-W-460478) which were delivered. The major difference between the U-4044 and the U-4144-T was the powerplant which was an Autocar D358. Installed at the end of U-4044 production, it was an engine with a capacity of 358 cubic inches (5,868 cc) rated at 100 bhp at

Below: Under some camouflage, a U-4044 and its Air Force 5-ton Instrument Shop Semitrailer, near Charleville in Australia, July 12, 1942. (U.S. Army Air Forces 21335 A. C.)

2,600 rpm without modification to the vehicle's general features. But the range was not followed up after 1941. The vehicles produced by Autocar and General Motors (the AFKX-502 intended for towing the cavalry trailers) were no longer ordered.

The Army's needs and ideas directed production toward the 4/5-ton 4x4 Truck Tractor.

U-5044

U-5044 was classified in the 4x4 5-ton category. This extrapolation enabled the Army to obtain a road vehicle with a payload double that of its forerunners, and with offroad capability as well. 97 vehicles were ordered and delivered in 1941 as part of contract W-398-QM-8687 (USA-W-51313 to USA-W-51409). Three parts of the truck were changed: a big protective cast-iron grille placed in front of the radiator grille including the headlights, only one spare tire, and the engine was reinforced. Now an Autocar D377, it equipped the U-5044s with a capacity of 377 cubic inches (6,180 cc) rated at 100 bhp at 2,400 rpm.

Above: The U-5044 was nothing but a U-4044 reclassified as a 5-ton truck. Among the few modifications were this large cast-iron grid in front of the radiator grille and the headlights. (U.S. Army SC-123885)

Center: Behind its radiator was a new, more flexible engine and only one spare wheel on the back of the cabin. In the Signal Corps, the U-5044 was given the name Truck K-32 for towing the SCR-770 radar. But even when used for this, it was quickly declared obsolete and replaced by the 4/5-ton 4x4 truck. (U.S. Army SC-124699)

Below: This U-4044 and its F2A 2,000-gallon 6-ton Fuel Servicing Semitrailer refuels a Curtiss C-46 ready to take off from India toward China, March 1945. (U.S. Army Air Forces A-35865 A.C.)

Field Bakeries

Above: Fort Meade, Maryland in September 1941, the Quartermaster Corps is testing this field bakery. Towing the outfit is an Autocar U-5044. (U.S. Army SC-123637)

Center: Called the Mobile Field Bakery, the trailers were twin 6-ton semitrailers coupled together, the second resting on a dolly. The first post was for preparing the bread dough and the second for the baking. (U.S. Army SC-123634)

Right: Such an installation could produce 4,000 loaves in 24 hours alone. On the front right of the first trailer, under the worktable, was a generator set that supplied the electricity needed including that for the kneading trough. A 250-gallon (950-liter) water tank was incorporated into the outfit. Fort Sheridan, July 1941. (ACME C-235524)

GMC CCKW-352 Hybrids

This category included the cargo trucks adapted in the field by the Ordnance units to tow the voluminous technical semitrailers.

Despite the number of all sorts of vehicles, and particularly the semitrailer tractors, certain units of the Ordnance Department managed to reconcile the two transport theories: a mix of the tractors being available for several trailers on the one hand, and the vehicles used for a single purpose on the other. Faced with a need for big mobile magazine-workshop trucks, there was no truck with enough inside space, and only a big trailer could take such a volume. But from an administrative point of view, no standard tractor could be assigned to this single task. To solve this problem, the GMC CCKWs were present at all levels and were transformed into workshop or office semitrailer tractors.

Right: The fittings inside the Machine Shop Trailer where five or six men could work comfortably. (U.S. Army SC-133262)

Below: CCKWX-353 (short chassis) Machine Shop of the Motor Maintenance Office at Fort Binning, March 14, 1942. The truck no longer has its transversal fuel tank and its two spare wheels; it has acquired a fuel tank inside the right-hand longeron which meant moving the battery and creating a slot in the bottom of the cabin. The semitrailer was of the 3-ton van type with electric brakes, an added side door, and window to make it a comfortable workshop. (U.S. Army SC-133269)

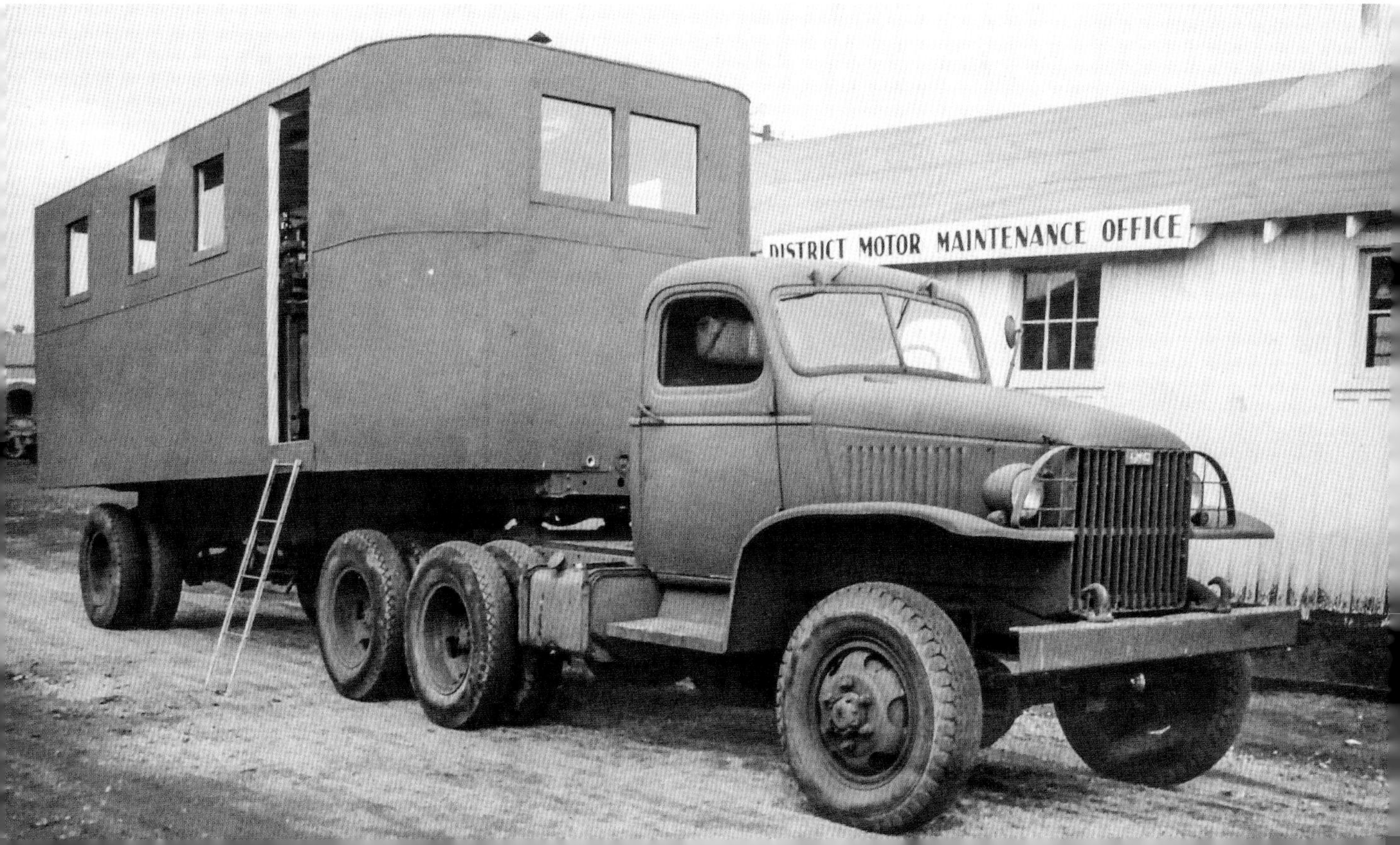

It was particularly the short wheelbase version of the CCKW-352 that was modified.

There were no limits or special modification plans and each unit carried out its own according to its needs and its availabilities. Some main trends appeared however: each vehicle received a compressor to supply the air needed for the trailers, together with an air reservoir. They were all old cargo vehicles whose body was replaced by the towing fifth wheel. When the transversal fuel tank on the short chassis was not retained, it was replaced by that from the long chassis fitted just in front of the rear tandem wheels on the left-hand or right-hand side with, if needed, a cutout in the bottom of the cabin. Incidentally, this type of operation was also carried out on the US6 Studebakers.

Above: This CCKW-352-A2 has kept its general features, the compressed-air intakes come out vertically from the chassis, the line of the exhaust has been modified, and the vehicle has 8.25x20 10-ply tires. Despite all the changes, the truck has exceptionally held onto its original registration number (USA-483403) which makes it part of the order for 600 cargo vehicles. (U.S. Army Signal Corps)

Left: Rarer is this canvas-topped version of the CCKW-352-A1 whose air tank in front of the wheels can be seen on the left-hand side. The rear lights as well as the electricity plug have been repositioned on the last crossmember of the chassis, which has lost its two stoppers as this happened often. (U.S. Army SC-279257)

Below: India, 1942, during the unloading of a sea convoy delivering supplies for the USSR. The CCKW-352-A2 has hardly undergone any transformations except for the change to the exhaust pipe and the installation of a fifth wheel. (U.S. Army SC-147440)

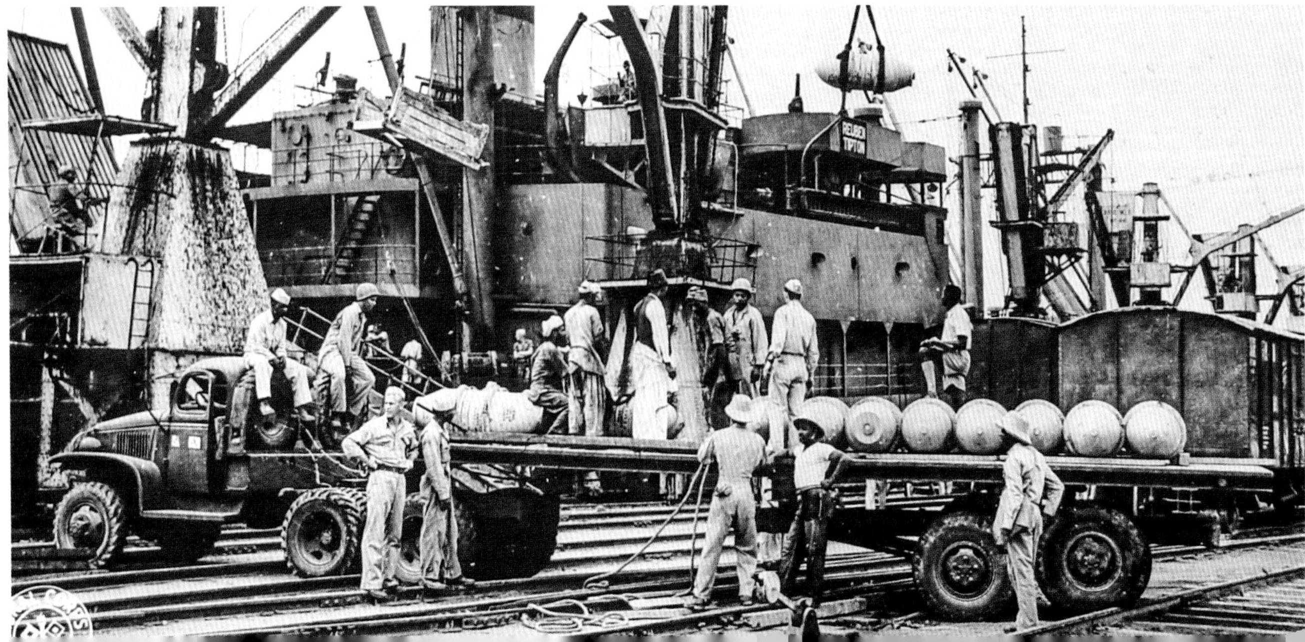

Above and left: The 53rd Quartermaster Company has built this Carburation and Ignition Trailer to work on electric and carburation components. The new fuel tank has been given a new spout and a protective floor. A spare wheel was installed behind the cabin as well as all the connections for the trailer. (U.S. Army SC-135283-85)

Left: Inside view of the Carburation and Ignition Trailer fitted out and customized. (U.S. Army SC-135282)

Right: CCKW-352-81 or a short GMC chassis with a Split winch and mechanics by Timken-Detroit. The A suffix probably designated a version without a winch whereas in place of the 1, a 2 would designate Banjo mechanics from Chevrolet. As each time with this kind of transformation, installing a fuel tank that was different from the truck model, a cutout had been made at the bottom of the cabin so it would not be too close to the rear wheels. (U.S. Army SC-135525)

Left: This ensemble designated as Quartermaster Parts Trailer is a mobile spare parts magazine. (U.S. Army SC-135526)

Below, left: The sides of the trailer were fitted out with shelf cupboards with removable doors. Each column was referenced by a letter of the alphabet and each rack was numbered. (U.S. Army SC-135523)

Below, right: At the back, just behind the only window, is a desk for keeping the inventory up to date and above all for consulting the technical manuals of which an example of each vehicle is available. (U.S. Army SC-135524)

The Shape

Based on two main longerons and six crossmembers, the outfit had a 145-inch (368.3-cm) wheelbase. The tractor was 87 inches (220.98 cm) high in the hardtop version, 88 inches (223.52 cm) wide, and 230 inches (584.2 cm) long. It weighed 9,030 lb net (4,100 kg); the CCKW could tow semitrailers weighing a maximum of 20,000 lb (9,080 kg) but could carry no more than 6,600 lb (2,996 kg) on the tractor's fifth wheel. The vehicle's braking system was the hydraulic type.

Above: Another interesting version is this truck tractor and its workshop trailer. The truck was a CCKW-352-1 where the whole fuel-supply system has been modified and the tank relocated on the left-hand longeron. (U.S. Army SC-133263)

Left: Building 6x6 tractors which were initially vehicles from the 2½-ton range, was not restricted to the GMC CCKW only. Here a Studebaker US6-U1 which has the advantage of being a 6x6 and not a 6x4 compared with the brand's tractors. (U.S. Army Signal Corps)

These modifications in the field took on unexpected profiles as here with this Diamond T Cargo which has become a truck tractor to evacuate the fuselage of a B-24. The 13th Engineer Combat Battalion of the 7th Infantry Division, at Okinawa, April 1945. (Private Collection)

The Mechanics

Using 7.50x20 8-ply tires, the CCKW-352 had two types of mechanics.

Initially designed on Split-type differentials from Timken-Detroit for reasons of availability, it was also allocated Banjo differentials from Chevrolet. The engine was a GMC 270 in a single block housing six pistons. This ensemble with culverted valves had a capacity of 269.5 cubic inches (4,418 cc) rated at 104 bhp at 2,750 rpm. It was water cooled with a radiator made up of vaned tubes and a water pump located on the front of the engine block, ventilation being by means of a five-bladed fan to increase the cooling of its 23 quarts (21.7 liters) which constituted the cooling circuit.

Transferring the engine power was through a Chevrolet single dry-disk clutch, with a gearbox with five forward and one reverse gears. With these mechanics, a Zenith carburetor, an AC pump, and a 40-gallon (151.40-liter) gasoline tank giving it a range of some 306¼ miles (490 km) by itself and 243¾ miles (390 km) coupled with a full payload, it had an average gasoline consumption of between 7.65 mpg and 6.09 mpg, depending on the type of road surface, the driving conditions, and whether it was towing. All the electrics worked on 6 volts, from a single battery, most of the electrical systems being made by Delco Remy.

3

4/5-Ton Truck Tractor Category

This category of semitrailer tractors became the U.S. Army standard to the detriment of the earlier 2½-ton trucks which were no longer powerful enough, because of new strategies developed and extensive logistics support created based on specialized semitrailers. There were 21,974 4/5-ton 4x4 Truck Tractors delivered by three companies: the Autocar Company in Ardmore, Pennsylvania, the Federal Motor Truck Co., Michigan, and the White Motor Company in Cleveland, Ohio. Production of these vehicles was spread out between May 1941, when the first 66 units were delivered, and August 1945 with the last 136 examples accepted by the Army.

Three vehicle models were involved in this category: the Autocar U-7144-T, the Federal 94x43, and the White 444.

Autocar U-7144-T Tractors

The most-ordered version of the 4/5-ton Truck Tractor, 11,104 examples of the Autocar U-7144-T were delivered. In its form and use, it was not too different from the Federal 94x43, of which 8,119 examples were bought.

They were both planned for the same jobs but rarely worked together. As the mechanical side of things was different, the tractors were mixed as little as possible within the same unit.

Just like the Autocar trucks, 2,751 trucks with the same shape and the same elements were ordered from the White Motor Company.

The Autocar U-7144-T was therefore only slightly modified. The cabin modification also meant that the big rear work platform was modified. This latter, in one single all-metal piece in the first series, took up the whole width of the truck by covering the fuel tank on the left-hand side and the bottles of compressed air on the right-hand side, filling the fuel tank being through the floor by means of an opening located on the top of the tank. With the so-called open cab, only a small wooden floor

was made that did not protrude over the side of the chassis width, plus the structure offset upward covering the fuel tank, the filling spout being modified to become a more easily-accessible wide lateral cornet.

A worrying fact: in the orders, 1,344 U-7144-Ts were bought with registration numbers beginning with a 5 (for the 5-ton vehicles) whereas it should have been a 4. However, given the vehicle's extraordinary sturdiness and its underemployed capacity, this section of the production was ordered as a 5/6-ton Tractor, with 12.00x20 14-ply tires as the only modification, the brackets for the spare wheels having to be moved upward. As the mechanics were not at all modified by these adaptations, no special Technical Manual (TM) was published.

In the context of Lend-Lease, 98 examples were supplied, described as 4/5-ton Trucks, to France mainly (76 examples) and the United Kingdom (12); 133 units described as 5/6-ton went to the Allied armies, nine for the United Kingdom and 124 for France.

The American vehicles were classified with finesse and a subtle mix of mechanical elements.

Right: Holabird Proving Ground: presentation of the pre-series U-7144-T. It has not yet been fitted with its fifth wheel, but its silhouette is already well defined.

Below left: Typical fitting-out of the rear of the cabin with the spare tires installed with a wide bracket. It was not until the canvas roof arrived that this part of the truck was modified.

Below right: On the right-hand side, we can see the single compressed-air reservoir from the very beginning of the project. Unlike the U-8144-T Pontoon Truck Tractor, the U-7144-T was not equipped with a winch, giving it a very squat profile. (U.S. Army Signal Corps)

Right and center: The soft-top hood (open cab) equipped the last 5,705 trucks, or from chassis No. U-7144-T-A-5400 to chassis No. U-7144-T-A-11704. Photographed on June 25, 1945, this example belonged to the next-to-last contract. (U.S. Army ORD-3493)

Below: Reduced to its simplest expression, this open cab only allowed two seats to be installed, as with all the tractors with a forward cabin. (SNL G-510)

Bottom: All the drivers passed through Camp Lee, where the Quartermaster Corps had installed its Motor Training School and its difficult obstacle course in the middle of the forest. This U-7144-T is towing a 6-ton Semitrailer Van. (*U.S. Army News*)

The perfect illustration of the theory of using semitrailers. This Autocar has just positioned its load consisting of a 6-ton Repair Semitrailer and is setting off on a new mission. (U.S. Army Signal Corps)

The training terrain was very selective and left no room for distraction. (*U.S. Army News*)

U-7144-T Truck Production			
Quantity	Orders	Registration Numbers	Comments
957	W-398-QM-10141	461794–462750	414 delivered in 1941 and 543 in 1942
212		482421–482632	All delivered in 1942
13		482662–482674	All delivered in 1942
100	W-398-QM-10802	487221–487320	All delivered in 1942
1,750	W-670-ORD-3176	490699–492448	All delivered in 1942
40		4108532–4108571	All delivered in 1942
151	W-670-ORD-3181	4110585–4110735	All delivered in 1942
206		4113260–4113465	All delivered in 1942
4,009	W-670-ORD-3317	4430000–4434008	266 delivered in 1942, 2,795 in 1943 and 948 in 1944
668	W-670-ORD-3317	552805–553472	All delivered in 1944
676	ORD-36-034-304	572417–573092	All delivered in 1944
1,537		4601134–4602670	798 delivered in 1944 and 739 in 1945
710	ORD-36-034-2499	4836909–4837618	All delivered in 1945
75	ORD-36-034-5404	4992944–4993018	All delivered in 1945
Of a total of 11,104 U-7144-T truck tractors: 414 were delivered in 1941, 3,281 in 1942, 2,795 in 1943, 3,090 in 1944 and the last 1,524 in 1945.			

It was sometimes enough to modify one to obtain surprising results. In the case of the 4/5-ton classification (a ton corresponding to about 907.20 kg), the truck could take a theoretical payload of between 7,798 lb (3,628 kg) and 10,000 lb (4,536 kg), and its tractive power was 20,000 lb (9,080 kg). By becoming a 5/6-ton simply by changing its tires, the U-7144-T was able to take a load of between 10,000 lb (4,536 kg) and 12,000 lb (5,443 kg) and its tractive power went up to 30,000 lb (13,620 kg) which meant it was a vehicle for two different uses: a medium and a heavy tractor.

The Shape

The Autocar U-7144-T was a COE-type truck and a technical part with a fifth wheel at the rear. Based on a chassis with two main longerons and five crossmembers, this outfit had two differentials with a wheelbase of 134.5 inches (341.63 cm). Built with a hardtop cabin for the 5,399 first vehicles then

Recovering a German bus trailer, France, September 12, 1944. (U.S. Army SC-194082)

New Caledonia, April 3, 1943, the 13th Air Depot Group has just recovered the remains of a crashed P-38 fighter. The convoy used chainsaws to advance through the jungle. The U-7144-T was coupled to a 25-foot Type C-2 Semitrailer. (U.S. Army Air Force, 71623 A.C.)

with a soft top for the next ones, the tractor was 112¾ inches high (286.39 cm) in its closed cabin configuration; the soft-top version enabled it to gain some 19 inches (about 50 cm) for transport by sea. It was 95 inches (241.3 cm) wide and 203½ inches (516.89 cm) long.

It weighed in all 12,360 lb (5,611 kg); the U-7144-T could tow semitrailers with a maximum weight of 20,000 lb (9,080 kg) but not take more than 8,950 lb (3,927 kg) on the tractor's fifth wheel. The braking system, working also for the trailers or the haulage, was of the compressed-air type—the Westinghouse Automotive Air Brake System. It was fed by a two-cylinder compressor driven directly by the engine; the air produced was stocked in the two cylindrical T-shaped tanks on the right-hand longeron on the chassis.

The pre-series vehicles as well as an unknown number of the first examples delivered only had one bottle, also located at the same place. Quick-fit fixtures for the trailer's brakes were located directly behind the cabin.

An interesting sand-yellow camouflaged version with white stars on a blue background. This configuration was present at John Payne Airfield, near Cairo, Egypt, in November 1943. (U.S. Army Air Forces, A-80727 A.C.)

Above: On the big USAAF installations, it was current to use semitrailer tractors well above their theoretical capacity, as here in tandem with an F-1A 4,000-gallon Fuel Servicing Semitrailer with its loaded weight of 43,717 lb (19,830 kg) with a carryover of 28,091 lb (12,742 kg) on the fifth wheel, almost double what was intended for the U-7144-T. Normally it was a tractor in the 7½-ton category that should have been used and not a vehicle of the 4/5-ton type. (U.S. Army Air Forces, 80727 A.C.)

Center: Using the vehicle in overcapacity was not always a profitable solution. Despite the Air Force's flat facilities, weather conditions could make the fields difficult, and the magnificent natural agility of these tractors was therefore no longer an advantage. (U.S. Army Air Forces, 50836 A.C.)

Below: The ideal load for the U-7144-T consisted of an F-2 2,000-gallon, 6-ton Gasoline Tank Semitrailer or as here, the F-2A, 310th Bomber Group, Algeria, North Africa, March 4, 1943. (U.S. Army SC-168299)

The Mechanics

Using 9.00x20 10-ply tires, the U-7177-T rested on two Timken-Detroit differentials, the F-2090-W for the front and the R-2090-W for the rear, both being of the double reduction type. The vehicle was powered by a Hercules RXC gasoline engine, consisting of a single block housing six pistons. This ensemble had a capacity of 529 cubic inches (8,700 cc), rated at 131 bhp at 2,300 rpm. It was water cooled, with a radiator made up of vaned tubes and a water pump located on the front of the engine block; ventilation was by means of a six-bladed fan to increase the cooling of its 40 quarts (37.84 liters) which constituted the cooling circuit.

Above: For many weeks, activity in the port of Antwerp was unbridled, and the large quantity of supplies to be transshipped from the boats needed an uninterrupted round of trucks. This Autocar was one of the 1,344 examples with a special registration number beginning with the number 5. (U.S. Army Signal Corps)

Left: The 10-ton Stake & Platform (S&P) Semitrailer was the one most used for merchandise. Modular as needed, it was perfectly adapted to the U-7144-T provided that running conditions were not too chaotic. On the road, the tractor worked as an 8/10-ton instead of a 4/5-ton offroad. (U.S. Army SC-201715)

Transferring the engine drive through a single dry-disk W.C. Lippe clutch was by means of a UU Autocar gearbox with five forward and one reverse gears, and a T-76-2Timken-Detroit transfer box which engaged the front differential, transforming the 4x2 into a 4x4. With these mechanics, a Zenith carburetor, an AC pump, and a 60-gallon (227.12-liter) fuel tank, it had a range of between 540 miles (869 km) by itself and 198 miles (319 km) coupled with the maximum payload which the U-7144-T was able to tow, or a consumption rate of 9 mpg or 4.95 mpg, this consumption varying with the type of road, the running conditions, and the configuration—whether towing or not.

All the electrical system worked on 6 volts from two 6-volt batteries set up in parallel, except for

Men and cartage suffered along the major supply routes across France and Belgium, like the Red Ball Express or the ABC Route. Depending on the official captions, ABC had a double meaning: either Antwerp–Brussels–Charleroi or American–British–Canadian—the armies resupplied from the port in Antwerp. (U.S. Army SC-201726)

The supply center of the 13th Traffic Regulation Group, at Saint-Denis, near Paris, a short while after the war. (U.S. Army Signal Corps)

Right: March 13, 1944, in the Ordnance Depot in Ashchurch, England, Private Charles Boudreau is carrying out the administrative check of this lot of Autocar truck tractors. The registrations have been repainted in big, white characters. (U.S. Army SC-314269)

Below left: Everything was a question of balance for this exceptional transport. Reykjavik, Iceland in September 1944, an Engineers' unit has to move its installations. With the available materiel, it was easier to move the prefabricated buildings in toto than dismantling them. The rigors of the weather have forced the crew to build a homemade hardtop cabin. (U.S. Army SC-201715)

Below right: Disembarking on a Japanese beach for this ensemble consisting of a 4/5-ton with a special registration number and its F-1A 4,000-gallon Fuel Servicing Semitrailer. (U.S. Army Signal Corps)

starting the engine which worked from a 12-volt starter. It was thanks to the electrical circuit of the ignition contactor, which alone was fed by the two batteries in series via an electromagnetic contactor, that this differentiation was possible. Most of the electrical parts were made by Delco-Remy.

Federal 94x43 Tractors

8,119 examples of another 4/5-ton truck tractor, the Federal 94x43, were delivered. In its form and its use, it was not very different from the Autocar U-7144-T and the White 444.

The Federal 94x43 only underwent a few changes during its production. Changing to a soft-top cabin meant modifying the big rear work platform. This—in one piece and all metal in the first series—took up the whole width of the chassis whereas the top of the reservoir was protected by a rack letting the filling nozzle through it vertically. Changing to the C model moved the latter to a forward position on the side of cabin, becoming a large lateral cone which was more easily accessible.

The first 94x43s, like all vehicles from the beginning of the 1940–41 production, came from the civilian series, with their components and a high degree of finish. 870 examples were ordered; these first 4/5-ton 4x4 truck tractors received the suffix with their builder's type. The second contract was made when the first significative modifications appeared. While the hardtop cabin was retained, the dashboard instrumentation was standardized by adopting military-type dials, the work platform behind the cabin was no longer nonslip metal—it was now made of wood as was the protective platform on the top of the reservoir supports. 1,948 examples of the 94x43 were ordered.

Most of the 94x43 were C types. Rationalizing sea transport and steel were at the basis of the new soft top which equipped the 5,301 other vehicles of this type.

Photographed directly on the forecourt of the factory, this pre-series vehicle gives a good idea of the stature of the 94x43, and a view of its battery box and the tool case. (Federal Motor Co. ref. 10316)

On this Federal 94x43 from the first series, the tank's filling nozzle was vertical through the little protective metal plate. (U.S. Army SC-170531)

When the appearance was overhauled, the truck nose lost its metallic pennant with the builder's logo; the left-hand spare wheel, which was in fact present for the twinning of the front axle, disappeared but it was still possible to fix it. One of the particularities of the beginning of production of this third version was that at least one example was built with a winch, certainly an interesting solution but in the case of the 4/5-ton tractors, it was not selected. It is also worth noting that, just as with the Autocar U-7144-T, 1,874 examples were given a registration number beginning with the 5 of the higher category.

The protuberance on the vehicle nose formed a crest bearing the brand name which was also the access hatch of the radiator cap. (Private Collection)

The Shape

The Federal 94x43 was a COE-type truck and a technical part with a fifth wheel at the rear. Based on a chassis with two main longerons and five crossmembers, this outfit rested on two differentials with a wheelbase of 134⅜ inches (341.31 cm). Built with a hardtop cabin for the first 2,818 vehicles then with a soft top for the next ones, the tractor was 109 inches high (276.86 cm) in the first case; the soft-top version enabled it to gain some 19 inches (about 50 cm) for transport by sea. It was 95.5 inches (242.57 cm) wide and 203 inches (515.62 cm) long.

Weighing in all 12,110 lb (5,498 kg), the U-7144-T could tow semitrailers with a maximum weight of 20,000 lb (9,080 kg) but could not take more than 8,650 lb (3,927 kg) on the tractor's fifth wheel. The braking system, working also for the trailers or the haulage, was of the compressed-air type—the Westinghouse Automotive Air Brake System. It was fed by a two-cylinder compressor driven directly by the engine; the air produced was stocked in two cylindrical tanks, one on the left longeron behind the fuel tank and the other transversally across the chassis in front of the rear wheels.

Federal Motor Truck Company 94x43 Production			
Quantity	Orders	Registration Numbers	Comments
680	W-398-QM-8981	428590 to 429269	All delivered in 1941 (Model 94x43A)
190		457287 to 457476	All delivered in 1941 (Model 94x43A)
1,948	W-374-ORD-2749	4113609 to 4115556	All delivered in 1942 (Model 94x43B)
1,910	W-374-ORD-2762	4355084 to 4356993	100 delivered in 1942, 1,751 in 1943 and 59 in 1944 (Model 94x43C)
85		4416133 to 4416217	All delivered in 1944 (Model 94x43C)
345	W-374-ORD-6496	554042 to 554386	All delivered in 1944 (Model 94x43C)
1,529		569623 to 571151	All delivered in 1944 (Model 94x43C)
855		4603171 to 4604025	615 delivered in 1944 and 240 in 1945 (Model 94x43C)
86		4835260 to 4835345	All delivered in 1945 (Model 94x43C)
430		4837619 to 4838048	All delivered in 1945 (Model 94x43C)
61	ORD-20-018-10419	4990745 to 4990805	All delivered in 1945 (Model 94x43C)
Of a total of 8,119 Truck Tractor 94x43s: 870 were delivered in 1941, 2,048 in 1942, 1,751 in 1943, 2,633 in 1944, and the last 817 in 1945.			

Quick-fit fittings for the trailer brakes were located directly behind the cabin.

The Mechanics

Using 9.00x20 10-ply tires, the Federal 94x43 rested on two Timken-Detroit differentials, an F-2090-W for the front and an R-2090-W at the rear, both being of the double reduction type. The vehicle was powered by a Hercules RXC gasoline engine in a single block housing six pistons. With a capacity of 529 cubic inches (8,700 cc), it was rated at 131 bhp at 2,300 rpm. It was water cooled with a radiator made up of vaned tubes and a water pump located on the front of the engine block, ventilation being by means of a six-bladed fan to increase cooling its 50 quarts (47.3 liters) which constituted the cooling circuit.

Transferring the engine drive with a single dry-disk W.C. Lippe clutch was by means of a 326 VO Clark gearbox with five forward and one reverse gears, and a Timken-Detroit T-76 two-stage transfer box which also engaged the front differential, transforming the 4x2 into a 4x4.

With these mechanics, a Zenith carburetor, an AC pump, and a 60-gallon (227-liter) fuel tank, the vehicle had a range of 491 miles (830 km) by itself or 180 miles (290 km) hitched up with the full payload the 94x43 could carry, a consumption rate of between 3 mpg and 8.18 mpg, this consumption varying with the type of road, the running conditions, and the configuration—whether towing or not. All the electrical system worked on 6-volts

Below: Switching to the soft-top cabin gave rise to the 94x43C version. The truck kept its main characteristics. It was given a new fuel tank and the drive blackout light on the left-hand wing. (U.S. Army Signal Corps)

Above: The few examples of the GMC AFKX-502 and the general rationalization meant that the 94x43 became the truck tractor assigned to the 6-ton Combination Animal & Cargo Semitrailer of the cavalry units. (U.S. Army SC-121585)

Right and below left: England, January 1944: endless maneuvers preparing for the invasion of Europe. From two different angles, the same 93x43C, registration number USA-4355380, called *Marcella*, followed by a 94x43B with a hardtop cabin. (U.S. Army SC-280135/136)

Below right: Switching to soft-top cabins gave the men the possibility of using an antiaircraft M66 ring mount machine gun. Very much later, a special kit was created for the 94x43As and 94x43Bs which was called the M-60. (U.S. Army SC-280131)

with a positive earth from two 6-volt batteries set up in parallel, except for starting the engine which worked with a 12-volt starter. It was thanks to the electrical circuit of the ignition contactor, which alone was fed by the two batteries in series via an electromagnetic contactor, that this differentiation was possible. Most of the electrical parts were made by Auto-Lite.

Above: Like all the tractors in the 4/5-ton category, the Federal 94x43 could be used with a considerable number of different trailers. Hitched up to an F2A 6-ton 2,000-gallon Gasoline Tank Semitrailer, the transfer was carried out via a 1-ton Fuel Servicing Trailer which had the advantage of having multi-gasoline pistols and of being able to calibrate the pressure for filling jerrycans since the F-2A's equipment was too powerful for this operation. (U.S. Army Signal Corps)

Below left: ABC Route in Belgium, in one of the numerous maintenance workshops all along the route. This example was one of the 1,874 Federal 94x43s to have been given a registration number beginning with the number 5. (U.S. Army SC-201225)

Below right: March 1944 in an English port. A Lockheed P-38 is being transported on a platform towed by a Federal 94x43. (U.S. Army Air Forces B-50295 A.C.)

White 444 Tractors

2,751 examples of this none-too-current version of the 4/5-ton Truck Tractor were built by the White Company and did not differ visually from Autocar's U-7144-T.

Registered as USA-4771531, this White 444 is identical to those produced later by Autocar, including the front hooks for towing replaced by shackles. All these 444s were the same shape and had the same soft-top cabin. (J.M. Boniface Collection)

It is difficult to define this production administratively. Given the nominative order made to the White Motor Co., it was not however any old sub-contract: this one could classify these supplies to the Army as sharing the patent or the license, with the express demand made by the authorities not to add a third model of truck in this category. Using the same constituent elements with another builder enabled production to be increased without adding to the number of models.

The enormous advantage of this practice was to enable maintenance operations to be perfectly consistent, components being interchangeable, and the stock of parts being reduced.

White Model 444-T Truck Production			
Quantity	Orders	Registration Numbers	Comments
2,000	ORD-33-019-973	4771379 to 4773378	1,510 delivered in 1944 and 490 in 1945
417		4834843 to 4835259	All delivered in 1945
334		4838049 to 4838382	All delivered in 1945
Of a total of 2,751 examples: 1,510 were received in 1944 and the last 1,241 examples in 1945.			

The Parts List drew a parallel between the references of the two manufacturers (White and Autocar). However, there was a minor difference between the two vehicles. They did not weigh the same: the U-7144-T weighed 12,360 lb (5 611.40 kg) and the White 444 weighed 12,560 lb (5 702.24 kg), a difference of 200 lb (90.80 kg).

Above: Winter 1944/45, lined up waiting for delivery to the Army in the White Company transfer zones are Truck Tractors 444. All that is missing is the application of the registration number for them to be complete. (J.M. Boniface Collection)

Below: Registered as USA-4771799 and USA-4771894, these two White 444s are being loaded in the port of Antwerp in March 1945. Both are hitched up to a 10-ton S&P Semitrailer. (U.S. Army SC-201718)

Right: A traditional scene before any departure: Private Douglas Doderer hands the driver, Thomas F. Tadlock, his road map with the details of his load and his destination. The registration number USA-4771690 was a White Tractor. (U.S. Army SC-201272)

Below: Coming out of the Motor Center Truck Pool in Tokyo in June 1952, this White 444 resumed service during the Korean War. (U.S. Army SC-201722)

Semitrailers Specific to the 4/5-Ton 4x4 Tractors

These semitrailers were used for almost all the Army's needs and were mainly intended to be towed by the 4/5-ton category of truck tractors made by Autocar and Federal.

From 1941, deliveries to the Army of the big semitrailers began. They were technical materiel which consisted of three main categories: the Signal Corps trailers, the Quartermaster trailers, and the Aviation trailers. They all had a point in common in that they were all fitted with a braking system which functioned with compressed air. Given the range of the suppliers, trailers of the same type might have small differences on the outside, either the covering or the type of the openings while being used for the same purpose. Some models like the Carryall or flatbed semitrailers were delivered in small numbers and for a limited use by the Corps of Engineers.

Left: For the Laundry Van Semitrailer, various inside fittings were added. Here, an assembly with a simple laundry and a spin-dryer. (U.S. Army SC-123340)

Bottom: Camp San Luis Obispo in California, 1943. Two Laundry Van Semitrailers have just been delivered. By their shape, they are identical to the Sterilizer & Bath Semitrailers. On the rear of the sides are removable ladders to access the roof and the positioning of the chimneys. (U.S. Army SC-167944)

Quartermaster Semitrailers

6-Ton (10-Ton Gross) Laundry Van Semitrailer

Of primordial use for the soldiers' well-being, this laundry trailer was an outfit with four big side openings whose horizontal panels enabled the floor surface and the roofing to be increased, the rear part of the trailer opening in the same way. Various fittings were made which depended on the job and the size of the unit which was to use it. There were complete laundry services with washing, spinning, and drying facilities or models with separate tasks like calendering and dry cleaning.

Although these semitrailers were intended to work autonomously for small itinerant units, like platoons which moved from division to division, they were generally grouped together within companies which increased the configuration and was more effective.

Intended only for washing clothes, bed linen, and health-service linen, 1,335 examples were delivered from four different builders:

- The Gramm Company supplied 992 examples (Model DF-75, USA-0101832 to USA-0102823)
- The Lufkin Company supplied 302 examples (Model D-1345, USA-017418 to USA-0174419).
- The Trailmobile Company supplied four examples (Model B-346H, USA-039245 to USA-039248).
- The Timpte Company supplied 37 examples under the designation Model T-8.

Top: Lighter equipment for this dry-cleaning version. Note the adjustable legs which enabled the panels to be kept horizontal to increase the work area. (U.S. Army Signal Corps)

Center: October 1944 on Guadalcanal, the 458th Quartermaster Laundry Company of the 525th QM Group was assigned to a hospital's laundry. It has parked its four semitrailers in battery. (U.S. Army SC-200268)

Bottom: The Quartermaster SL-564 depot in Italy assembled 12 Laundry Van Semitrailers, all linked by a system of gangplanks which made moving the chariots of laundry easier. In this configuration, 1,201 lb (545 kg) of clothes were dealt with in an hour. (U.S. Army SC-205030)

These were supplied as four batches in 1941, 921 in 1942, and 410 in 1943.

These vans with single axles and with twin 9.00x20 10-ply wheels with a wheelbase of 214 inches (543.56 cm)—axis differential to the coupling point—had a total length of 269 inches (683.26 cm), width of 96 inches (243.84 cm), and height of 132 inches (335.28 cm). They weighed 8,007 lb (3,632 kg) empty and could take a maximum weight of 12,010 lb (5,448 kg). The distribution of the mass had the tractor's fifth wheel carry 7,383 lb (3,349 kg) and 12,634 lb (5,731 kg) on its axle, a distribution ratio of 37% to 63%.

Top: Prepared for sea transport, these Sterilizer & Bath Van Semitrailers are waiting to be convoyed to their destination. (U.S. Army Signal Corps)

Center and below: A report in the United States on the semi Trailmobile. This trailer's first purpose was to decontaminate men who had been in contact with chemical agents. But as combat gas was not used, they were assigned to washing and disinfecting the laundry, but also, thanks to their showers, to cleaning soldiers coming back from the front. The men took off their clothes and equipment which were placed in the autoclave at the same time as they went under the spray of a disinfection shower. Each wash consumed less than a liter of liquid. Clean clothes were handed out in a tent at the end of the circuit. (U.S. Army SC-123332/ SC-120060)

Above: Autocar U-7144-T and Refrigerator Van Semitrailer during maneuvers with the Quartermaster Corps (U.S. Army Signal Corps)

(10-Ton Gross) Sterilizer & Bath Van Semitrailer

Terrible memories of combat gas in 1917–18 led America to equip its troops with the means for decontaminating them. These trailers were intended for decontaminating men who had been in contact with chemical agents together with their equipment. Designed on the same basis as the laundry trailer, the Sterilizer & Bath Van Semitrailer had washing machines for washing the dirty uniforms and showers for the personnel.

There were 162 examples delivered from four different builders:

- The Hyde Company supplied 56 examples (Model 22-S, Reg. No. USA -0101726 to USA-0101783).
- The Strick Company supplied 53 examples (Model 400, USA-0101784 to USA-0101831; USA-0199147 to USA-0199151); (USA-0174720 to USA-0174768).
- The Trailmobile, one only (Model B-34-H, USA-039249).
- The Timpte Company with 37 examples of its T-8 Model.

These were supplied as one unit in 1941, 143 in 1942, and 18 in 1943.

These vans with single axles and twin 9.00x20 10-ply wheels had a wheelbase of 214 inches

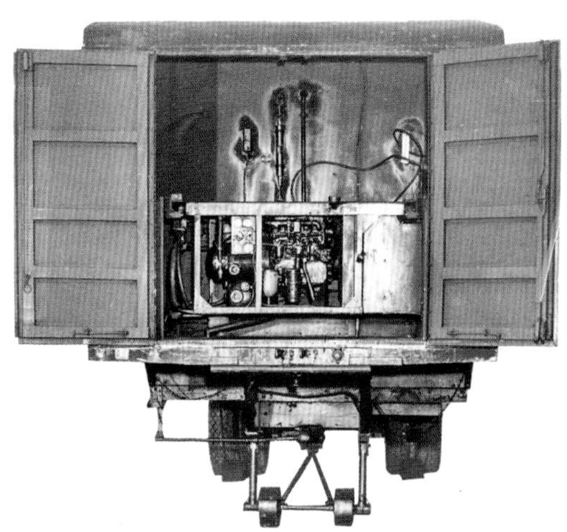

Bottom left: The double door on the front of the trailer gave access to the refrigeration machinery. It was an entirely independent installation with about 20 hours' self-sufficiency, depending on the climatic zone and the inside temperature to be maintained. (U.S. Army Signal Corps)

Bottom right: Covered entirely with smooth material, the interior had to be maintained to an irreproachable degree of hygiene. (U.S. Army SC-169491)

(543.56 cm)—axis differential to the coupling point—for a total length of 152 inches (685.8 cm), a width of 93¼ inches (236.86 cm), and a height of 138½ inches (351.79 cm). They weighed 9,508 lb (4,313 kg) empty and could take a maximum weight of 12,010 lb (5,448 kg). The distribution of the mass had the tractor's fifth wheel carry 9,008 lb (4,086 kg) and 12,511 lb (5,675 kg) on its axle, a distribution ratio of 42% to 58%.

The 5-Ton (10-Ton Gross) Refrigerator Van Semitrailer

Supplying perishable foodstuffs over long road distances was solved with this vehicle. The long, closed-in body was accessible by a double rear door. It consisted of two compartments: the first, for stocking foodstuffs, was refrigerated and lined with enameled sheets; the second was accessible from the front where the refrigeration machinery was kept. The inside was designed to be totally aseptic and perfectly clean hygienically. The sides and the floor were covered with a special finish so that bacteria had nothing to cling to; there was no corner with a right angle between horizontal and vertical surfaces—a configuration which made cleaning and disinfecting easier between trips. There were rails inserted into the ceiling to suspend the quarters of meat. Accessible by a double door at the front, the refrigeration group was entirely self-sufficient. Two companies shared the production of the refrigeration system: Waukashaw with its ACTU motor and Continental with its Y-69 model. They organized refrigerated transportation at temperatures between 32°F (0°C) and 54°F (12.2°C).

A total of 239 trailers were delivered by three manufacturers:

- The Hyde Company supplied 86 examples: Model KR-20, Reg. No. USA-0103080 to USA-0103165.
- The Trailmobile Company, 80 examples: Model TD-42, Reg. No. USA-049401 to USA-049406 and USA-0141570 to USA-0141643.
- The American Body Company, 73 examples, Model DF-73-R, Reg. No. USA-0141644 to USA-0141716.

These vans with single axles and twin 9.00x20 10-ply tires had a wheelbase of 188 inches (477.52 cm)—axle differential to the coupling point—for a

Below: A decontamination exercise on a refrigerated trailer from the beginning of production at the Quartermaster School at Fort Lee. The M2 Decontaminator Apparatus of the vehicle was only used for the limited surfaces that the crew had to touch. It enabled the job to be completed before going back to the tractor-trailer ensemble's adopted base. (U.S. Army Signal Corps)

Bottom: The 5-ton Stake & Platform Semitrailer in the Standard Nomenclature List. (SNL G-675)

Above: An experimental configuration for this Federal 94x43C, tested at the Aberdeen Proving Ground in May 1944. Lengthening the chassis to install a winch gave the truck a unique silhouette. The trailer is the 5-ton S&P Semitrailer. (U.S. Army ORD-A4273)

total length of 253.5 inches (643.89 cm), a width of 96 inches (243.84 cm), and a height of 126 inches (320.04 cm).

The vehicle weighed 14,713 lb (6,674 kg) empty and could take a maximum weight of 10,008 lb (4,540 kg). The distribution of the mass had the tractor's fifth wheel carry 11,918 lb (5,046 kg) and 13,598 lb (6,168 kg) on its axle, a distribution ratio of 45% to 55%.

These were supplied as six units in 1941, 200 in 1942, and 33 in 1943.

Right: Sydney, Australia, October 3, 1942, a Machine Records Unit has set up its materiel as a workstation behind a bank. (U.S. Army SC-172224)

The 5-Ton (10-Ton Gross) Stake & Platform (S&P) Semitrailer

These semitrailers, also called cargo, were assigned to transporting everyday supplies. Consisting of a platform and removable drop-sides, there were several configurations. There were 8,107 examples delivered, all called Model 516, coming from three different manufacturers:

- The Olson Company supplied 800 examples (USA-0735847 to USA-0736646).
- The Trailmobile Company, 6,399 examples (USA-0728647 to USA-0735045).
- The Truck Engineering Company, 908 examples (USA-0735047 to USA-0735846 and USA-0933448 to USA-0933555).

They appeared late and at the same time as the 4x2 H-542-9/M-425 International Harvester Truck Tractors (compare with the following chapter) which were officially intended for towing, but only on road surfaces.

They were delivered as follows: 5,975 examples in 1944 and 2,132 examples in 1945.

These vans with single axles and with twin 9.00x20 10-ply wheels had a wheelbase of 120 inches (304.8 cm)—axle differential to the coupling point—for a total length of 202 inches (513.08 cm), a width of 96 inches (243.84 cm), and a height of 104 inches (264.16 cm). It weighed 6,645 lb (3,015 kg) empty and could take a maximum weight of 10,008 lb (4,540 kg). The distribution of the mass had the tractor's fifth wheel take 7,006 lb (3,178 kg) and 9,649 lb (4,377 kg) on its axle, a distribution ratio of 42% to 58%

6-Ton (10-Ton Gross) Mobile Records Van Semitrailer

This denomination regrouped the semitrailers that were purely administrative, for managing official documents by the Adjutant General's Department. There were 276 examples delivered with two quite special appellations: 101 Administration Van Semitrailers and 175 I.B.M. Van Semitrailers.

Camp Young, November 23, 1942, the 4th Machine Records Unit using an Administration Van Semitrailer and an I.B.M. Van Semitrailer back-to-back. (U.S. Army SC-168173)

Parked two by two, they made up a Machine Records Unit. Their job in a headquarters (army corps, army, etc.) was to manage all the unit archives and their personnel using perforated cards.

These vans with single axles and twin 9.00x20 10-ply wheels had a wheelbase of 197 inches (500.38 cm)—axle differential to the coupling point—for a total length of 152 inches (685.8 cm), a width of 95¾ inches (243.2 cm), and a height of 140 inches (355.6 cm). It weighed 10,710 lb (4,858 kg) empty and could take a maximum weight of 12,010 lb (5,448 kg). The distribution of the mass had the fifth wheel of the tractor carry 9,008 lb (4,086 kg) at maximum weight and 13,658 lb (6,200 kg) on its axle, a distribution ratio of 39% to 61%.

Mobile Records Van Semitrailers Produced by Trailmobile

Quantity	Orders	Registration Numbers	Comments
16	W-398-QM-12398	098283 to 098330	Van Administration / Van I.B.M. All delivered in 1942
3	W-670-ORD-3302	0141561 to 0141569	Van Administration. All delivered in 1943
6			Van I.B.M. All delivered in 1942
1	W-670-ORD-3248	0319215	Van I.B.M. Delivered in 1943
11		0319216 to 0319248	Van Administration / Van I.B.M. All delivered in 1943
5	W-670-ORD-4359	0424757 to 0424771	Van Administration / Van I.B.M. All delivered in 1943
34	W-670-ORD- 36-034-409	0653099 to 0653163	Van Administration / Van I.B.M. All delivered in 1944
18		0798868 to 0798885	Van I.B.M. All delivered in 1944
6		0798886 to 0798891	Van Administration. 3 deliveries in 1944 and 3 in 1945
23		0837679 to 0837701	Van I.B.M. All delivered in 1944
13		0837702 to 0837714	Van Administration. All delivered in 1944
7	W-670-ORD- 36-034-3237	0847567 to 0847573	Van Administration. All delivered in 1945
14		0847553 to 0847566	Van I.B.M. All delivered in 1945
6	W-670-ORD- 36-034-3534	0871617 to 0871622	Van Administration. All delivered in 1945
18		0871599 to 0871616	Van I.B.M. All delivered in 1945

The Administration Van Semitrailer is nothing more than an office. (U.S. Army SC-168171)

The I.B.M. Van Semitrailer section had perforated card drives inside. The two trailers were air-conditioned, had a double door at the rear, and a skylight at the front. They were entirely self-sufficient, producing their own electricity. (U.S. Army SC-168174)

6-Ton Workshop Van Semitrailer

These three trailers which resembled each other on the outside dealt with clothing and equipment. They were entirely metal-bodied with three lateral windows, plus a door at the front and at the rear, with integrated lighting, passive ventilation, and additional heating. Depending on the builder, two external coverings were used: panels made of smooth metal on a structural frame, or self-supporting ribbed panels, this second configuration offering a negligeable weight saving of 100 lb (45.40 kg). These vans with single axles and twin 9.00x20 10-ply wheels had a wheelbase of 197 inches (500.38 cm)—axle differential to the coupling point—for a total length of 270 inches (685.8 cm), a width of 96 inches (243.84 cm), and a height of 132 inches (335.28 cm). Weighing 8,507 lb (3,859 kg) empty, they could take a maximum weight of 12,010 lb (5,448 kg). The distribution of the mass had the tractor's fifth wheel carry 8,456 lb (3,836 kg) and 12,059 lb (5,470 kg) on its axle, a distribution ration of 41% to 59%.

This equipment was grouped in the Quartermaster Salvage Repair Company.

Demonstration of a Salvage Repair Company exhibiting its new equipment. In order: a Textile Repair Van, a Shoe Repair Van, and a Clothing Repair Van. (U.S. Army Signal Corps)

Clothing Repair Van Semitrailer

Fitted with powerful sewing machines and all the consumables specific to the job, the Clothing Repair Semitrailers were made for repairing clothing. There were 131 delivered, coming from three different manufacturers. The Gentry Company supplied six examples (USA-0136291 to USA-0136296) designated Model R-22, the Rivers Company 30 examples (USA-0136231 to USA-0136260) designated Model GD-22-4, and finally, the Timpte Company 95 examples designated Model T-8. There were 36 units supplied in 1942 and 95 in 1943.

Textile Repair Van Semitrailer

Like the preceding models, the Textile Repair Semitrailers were intended for repairing canvas equipment (tents, etc.). There were 125 examples delivered by three different manufacturers. The Carter Company supplied 40 examples (USA-0136261 to USA-0136290 and USA-0177021 to USA-0177030) designated as Model C-15-531, the Utility Company 40 examples (taken from the series USA-0176811 to USA-0176910, the other 60 were simple vans) designated Model G-SW-4, and finally, the Timpte Company with 45 examples designated as the Model T-8. There were 18 units supplied in 1942 and 107 in 1943.

Shoe Repair Van Semitrailer

This shoe repair trailer carried out all the repair and maintenance work for footwear. There were 146 examples delivered by three different manufacturers. The Trailmobile Company supplied one example (USA-039244) designated as the Model TD-34-H, the Gerstenlager Company 30 examples (USA-0136201 to USA-0136230) designated as the

Top: Depending on the manufacturer, there were small visible differences: the size of the windows, the way the panels were built, smooth or structured, and the internal ventilation. But they all had three windows per side and two doors, front and back. (U.S. Army Signal Corps)

Center: A variant of the trailer, in the shape of the windows. (U.S. Army SC-138281)

Bottom: The Clothing or Textile Repair Vans only differed by the sewing machines and the consumables. All the machines were powered electrically from a generator installed at the rear on the left-hand side which means that these two models have a large aeration grille positioned at the bottom of the rear side of the trailer. (U.S. Army SC-123340)

Above: Five technicians could work without difficulty in the Shoe Repair Van Semitrailer. (U.S. Army SC-123336)

Left: 19 May 1943, a Quartermaster Salvage Repair Company is deployed in North Africa. On the left-hand side some Shoe Repair Van Semitrailers have been assembled; there does not seem to be any lack of work whereas on the right, a Textile and Clothing Repair Van Semitrailer forms an ensemble. (U.S. Army SC-184892)

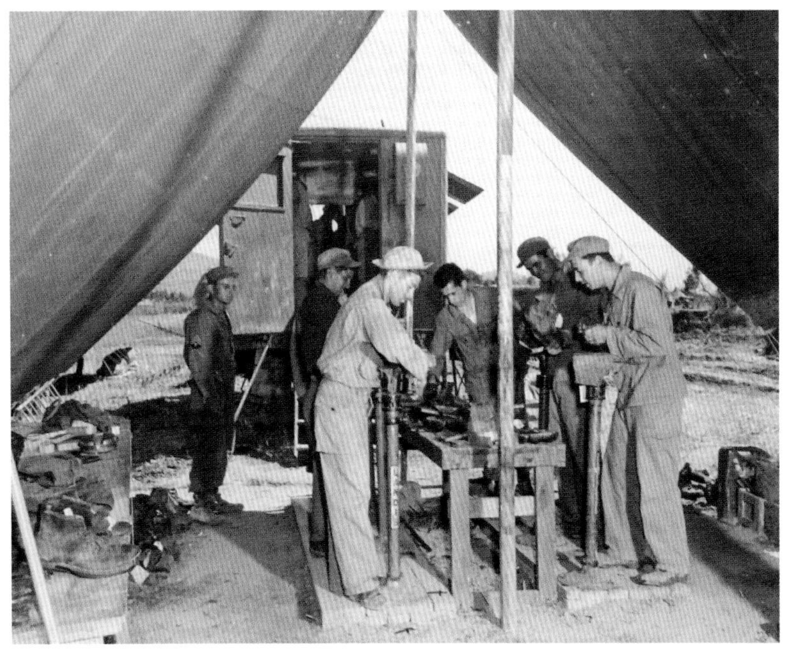

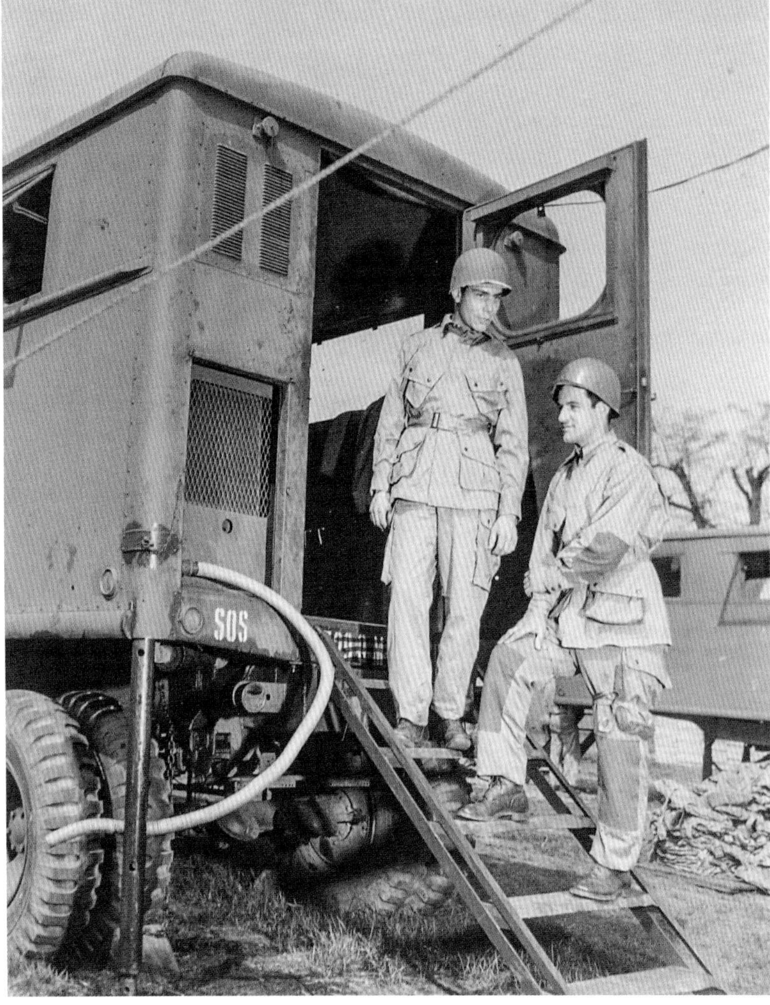

Model W-8125 (100 were taken from the series USA-0176592 to USA-0176810, the other 119 were simple vans, designated as the Model W-8120, and finally, the Timpte Company supplied 15 examples designated as the Model T-8. One unit was supplied in 1941, 26 in 1942, and 119 in 1943.

Tankers

6-Ton (10-Ton Gross) Water & Gas Tank Semitrailer

Two tanker semitrailers, for water or fuel, are included in this category, the 1,500-gallon Water Tank Semitrailers, of which 594 were found to have existed, delivered by the Columbus Steel Tank Co., and the 2,000-gallon Gas Tank Semitrailer of which 4,032 were made by eight different manufacturers and designated by two models, F2 and F-2A.

Above left: When the workload was intense and the trailer too small, the workshop and some of the tools were placed in a tent near the truck. Piombino region, Italy, July 10, 1944. (U.S. Army SC-313059)

Above right: There was no lack of repair work, especially resoling, in the 216th QM Co. of V Corps. The repaired boots are waiting to be collected by their owners' unit. (U.S. Army SC-123337)

Left: The Repair Trailers also worked on request, like resizing clothing. Here two paratroopers have just recovered their adjusted/reinforced clothing. (U.S. Army SC-314714)

Above: A rare shot of a 1,500-gallon Water Tank Semitrailer, towed here by a 94x42 Federal. The drinking water it has just loaded came from the Water Purification Truck in the background. (U.S. Army Signal Corps)

Center: This 1,500-gallon Water Tank Semitrailer has been given a recirculation ramp. In action on an Air Force terrain in Normandy, the water fixes the dust. (U.S. Army Signal Corps)

Below: New Guinea, May 1943. A Curtiss P-40 is being refueled from an F2 2,000-gallon Gas Tank Semitrailer. (U.S. Army Air Forces 79235 A.C.)

1,500-Gallon Water Tank Semitrailer

These tankers with single axles and twin 9.00x20 10-ply wheels had a wheelbase of 187 inches (475.38 cm)—axle differential to the coupling point—for a total length of 223 inches (566.42 cm), width 96 inches (243.84 cm), and height 90 inches (228.6 cm). Weighing 7,506 lb (3,405 kg) empty, they could take a maximum weight of 12,460 lb (5,652 kg). The distribution of the mass had the fifth wheel of the tractor carry 8,805 lb (3,994 kg) and the axle 10,761 lb (4 881 kg), a distribution ratio of 45% to 55%. They were equipped with a pump unit in the right-hand coffer; the inside was entirely enameled so it could take drinking water. Note that in the U.S. Army the Water Service was part of the Engineers.

F-2 2,000-Gallon Gas Tank Semitrailer

These tankers with single axles and with twin 9.00x20 10-ply wheels had a wheelbase of 161½ inches (410.2 cm)—axle differential to the coupling point—for a total length of 303 inches (769.62 cm), a width of 93 inches (236.22 cm), and a height of 102 inches (259.08 cm). Weighing 8,408 lb (3,814 kg) empty, they could carry a maximum weight of 12,412 lb (5,630 kg). The distribution of the mass had the fifth wheel of the tractor carry 9,808 lb (4,449 kg) and 11,009 lb (4,994 kg) on its axle, a distribution ratio of 47% to 53%. It was fitted with two motor pump groups, one at the rear, one on the side, and the fuel tank was entirely made of aluminum.

F-2A 2,000-Gallon Gas Tank Semitrailer

These tankers with single axles and with twin 9.00x20 10-ply wheels had a wheelbase of 161½ inches (410.2 cm)—axle differential to the coupling point—for a total length of 306 inches (777.24 cm), a width of 93 inches (236. 22 cm), and a height of 96 inches (243.84 cm). The weight limits were the same as for the previous version. It was fitted with a single motor pump group on the rear, and the tank was entirely made of steel.

F2 & F2A 2,000-Gallon 6-Ton Gas Tank Semitrailer Registration Numbers

Manufacturer	Quantity	Registration Numbers
Davis Welding	400 examples	0654525 to 0654724 / 0804276 to 0804475
Heil	2,326 examples	0718819 to 0719914 / 0636146 to 0636497 / 0808130 to 0809007
Independent Metal	250 examples	0655845 to 0656094
Keystone	250 examples	0655595 to 0655844
Krieger Steel	300 examples	0654725 to 0655024
Lufkin	200 examples	0803231 to 0803430
Progress	300 examples	0719915 to 0720214
Fruehauf	6 early examples delivered in 1941	

Noumea, refueling another Curtiss P-40. The F2 Semitrailer is towed here by an M2 Cletrac High Speed Tractor. (U.S. Army Air Forces 63261 A.C.)

Above: Filling an F2A, 2,000-gallon, Gas Tank Semitrailer, India, September 1944. (U.S. Army Air Forces 73493 A.C.)

Below: On a French road used by the Red Ball Express, an F2 towed by an Autocar U-7144-T. (U.S. Army SC-198959)

An Autocar 4/5-ton 4x4 Truck Tractor and a 6-ton Van Semitrailer, Australia, September 24, 1942. Both were destined to meet each other; the outfit formed by this tractor with a hardtop and the van semitrailer made for a very harmonious ensemble. (U.S. Army SC-169490)

6-Ton (10-Ton Gross) Van Semitrailer

Among all the types of semitrailers, the vans were in the end the simplest structures, their only job being to transport supplies safely. Made from 1941 to 1945 nonstop, 5,248 examples were delivered to the Army from 14 manufacturers, each of them having their little particularities. Two outside coverings were used, the smooth panels on a structural frame, and the self-supporting panels, without this changing the trailers' designation. The insides were covered with protective panels over two-thirds of the height, to protect the structure from impacts. Entirely removable, the rear consisted of three parts: one was the fold-down bottom tailgate, and the other two side-opening top leaves.

These vans with single axles and with twin 9.00x20 10-ply wheels had a wheelbase of 186¾ inches (474.35 cm)—axle differential to the coupling point—for a total length of 248 inches (629.92 cm), a width of 97 inches (246.38 cm), and a height of 131 inches (332.74 cm).

Weighing 7,506 lb (3,405 kg) empty, they could take a maximum weight of 12,010 lb (5,630 kg). The distribution of the mass had the tractor's fifth wheel take 6,746 lb (3,060 kg) and 12,771 lb (5,793 kg) on its axle, a distribution ratio of 34% to 66%. There were 241 units supplied in 1941, 1,886 in 1942, 1,747 in 1943, 1,018 in 1944, and 1,356 in 1945.

6-Ton Van Semitrailer Registration Numbers

Manufacturer	Quantity	Model	Registration Numbers
American Bantam	354 examples	STV-620	0803781 to 0803781 / 0802533 to 0802536
American Body	200 examples	DF-223-V	0457474 to 0457673
Carter	310 examples	C-15	0176911 to 0177020 / 0457074 to 0457273
Checker	610 examples	SVT-620	0804946 to 0805555
Doersey	100 examples	E-14	0457874 to 0457973
Gramm	411 examples	DF-75	0806406 to 0806816
Highway	975 examples	SKD-2181 & SKD-2215	0144469 to 0144917 / 0144918 to 0145322 / 121 unlisted
Kentucky	310 examples	4-Q-B	0176482 to 0176591 / 0457274 to 0457473
Olson	823 examples	LV-10	0315482 to 0315981 / 323 unlisted
Strick	350 examples	400-W	0456474 to 0456823
Timpte	200 examples	T-8	0457674 to 0457873
Utility	185 examples	G-SW-4	0456824 to 0457008
Trailmobile	241 examples	TD-34-H	043105 to 043272 / 049407 to 049469 / 054918 to 054927
Utility	60 examples	G-SW-4	From the series 0176811 to 0176910. The other 40 being Textile Repair Semitrailers
Gerstenslager	119 examples	W-8120	Taken from the series 0176592 to 0176810. The other 100 being Shoe Repair Semitrailers

Above left and right: Be they with smooth panels or with structured panels, these semitrailers were identified in the same way and intended for the same uses. Here it's a TD-34H by Trailmobile. (U.S. Army Signal Corps)

Left. Behind the cupboards of this spare parts van magazine, the insides were recovered with protective panels over two-thirds of the height. Entirely removable, the rear consisted of three parts, one the fold-down bottom tailgate, and the other two side-opening top leaves. (U.S. Army Signal Corps).

Below left: The vans were not intended for just any transport; this one has been loaded with mechanical parts for the Dodge ½-ton 4x4 truck including two engines. (U.S. Army Signal Corps)

Below right: The inside lining of the trailer shows how useful it was for protecting the panels. (U.S. Army Signal Corps)

Special 6-Ton Air Force Semitrailers

The U.S. Army Air Forces ordered their own technical trailers of which 898 examples were delivered by six different manufacturers. It was very round at the front, so they were well recognizable.

Instrument Shop Semitrailer

These workshops were fitted out for repairing, calibrating and maintenance of the aircraft flight instruments. Without any openings except the side doors, the inside is under positive pressure to prevent the slightest speck of dust or insect from entering and impairing the proper functioning of the mechanisms. These vans with single axles and with twin 9.00x20 10-ply wheels had a wheelbase of 284½ inches (722.63 cm)—axle differential to the coupling point—for a total length of 341 inches (866.14 cm), a width of 95½ inches (242.57 cm), and a height of 132 inches (335.28 cm). Weighing 19,451 lb (8,823 kg) empty, the distribution of the mass meant the fifth wheel of the tractor taking 9,726 lb (4,412 kg) and 9,724 lb (4,411 kg) on its axle, a distribution ratio of 50% to 50%.

Field Shop Repair Semitrailer

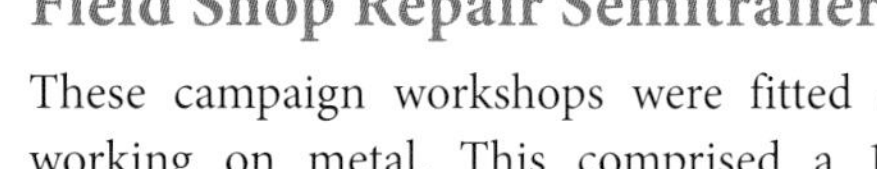

These campaign workshops were fitted out for working on metal. This comprised a 110-volt generator set, an oil heater, a turn, and a column drill, as well as all the necessary tooling. These van semitrailers with single axles and twin 9.00x20 10-ply wheels had a wheelbase of 290¾ inches (738.51 cm)—axle differential to the hitch-up point—for a total length of 363½ inches (920.75 cm), a width of 96 inches (243.84 cm), and a height of 134 inches (340.36 cm). Weighing 9,008 lb (4,086 kg) empty, they could take a maximum weight of 8,558 lb (3,882 kg). The distribution of the mass had the tractor's fifth wheel take 7,826 lb (3,550 kg) and 9,737 lb (4,417 kg) on its axle, a distribution ratio of 44% to 56%. They had three windows on each side and a door. On the front, a small grille door protected the machinery inside.

Photographic Laboratory Semitrailer

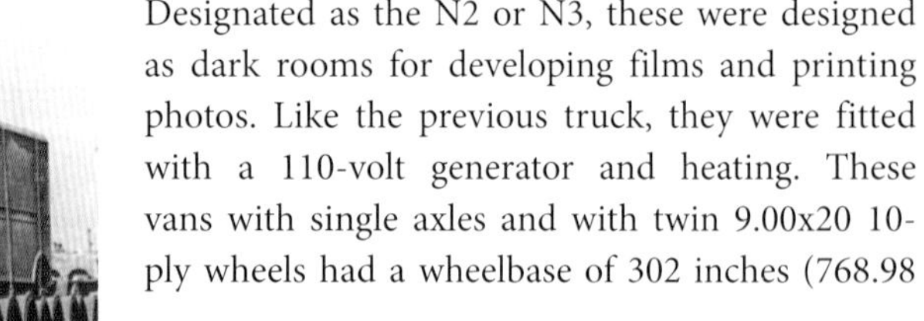

Designated as the N2 or N3, these were designed as dark rooms for developing films and printing photos. Like the previous truck, they were fitted with a 110-volt generator and heating. These vans with single axles and with twin 9.00x20 10-ply wheels had a wheelbase of 302 inches (768.98

Above: The 23rd Photographic Squadron lands in France, September 4, 1944. A Photographic Laboratory Semitrailer hitched to an Autocar U-7144-T leaving its LST. (U.S. Army signal Corps)

Left: Railway station in the Indian province of Assam, 1943. Two Instrument Shop Semitrailers are about to be unloaded. (U.S. Army Air Forces 68413 A.C.)

cm)—axle differential to the coupling point—for a total length of 361½ inches (918.21 cm), a width of 96 inches (243.84 cm) and a height of 127 inches (322.58 cm). Weighing 11,230 lb (5,230 kg) empty, they could take a maximum weight of 17,495 lb (7,936 kg). The distribution of the mass meant the tractor's fifth wheel took 13,011 lb (5,902 kg) and 16,014 lb (7,264 kg) on its axle, a distribution ratio of 44% to 56%. Grille-covered windows and a side door were the visible points of this trailer.

Technical Supply Semitrailer

A magazine for aircraft spare parts and accessories, this trailer with a generator, internal heating and mechanical ventilation had two side windows and access from the rear. These vans with single axles and twin 9.00x20 10-ply wheels had a wheelbase of 290 inches (738.51 cm)—axle differential to the coupling point—for a total length of 349½ inches (887.73 cm), a width of 96 inches (243.84 cm), and a height of 129 inches (327.66 cm). Weighing 10,595 lb (4,086 kg) empty, they could take a maximum weight of 4,253 lb (1,930 kg). The distribution of the mass had the tractor's fifth wheel take 5,804¾ lb (2,633 kg) and 7,456 lb (3,382 kg) on its axle, a distribution ratio of 56% to 44%.

Map Reproduction Semitrailer

This trailer assigned by the Engineers to the cartographic service had a different mount from the others but its design was identical and was always considered a 6-ton (10-ton Gross) Semitrailer.

Above: Working position for this Technical Supply Semitrailer, installed in the shelter of the trees on the Island of Oahu, Hawaii, April 1944. (U.S. Army Air Forces 58983 A.C.)

Below: In Italy, placed side by side, these two Photographic Laboratory Semitrailers enabled photographs to be developed and printed more rapidly by combining their potential. (U.S. Army Air Forces 58983 A.C.)

Bottom: This Field Shop Repair Semitrailer is waiting for its tractor to leave. (U.S. Army Signal Corps)

Although its tires had become 12.00x20 14-ply, this was so it could be coupled to 5/6-ton class tractors. It was equipped with a double side door and three windows.

The wheelbase was 284 inches (721.36 cm)—axle differential to the coupling point—for a total length of 350 inches (889 cm), a width of 97 inches (246.38 cm), and a height of 128 inches (325.12 cm). Weighing 23,521 lb (10,669 kg) empty, the distribution of the mass had the tractor's fifth wheel carry 8,007 lb (3,632 kg) and 15 513 lb (7,037 kg) on its axle, a distribution ratio of 34% to 66%.

Not being counted with the four previous semitrailers, this one was produced by Fruehauf; 43 examples were delivered, three in 1940, and the others in 1941, under the registration numbers USA-W-039471 to USA-W-039510, for the last 40.

USAAF 6-Ton Semitrailer Registration Numbers

Manufacturer	Quantity	Model	Registration Numbers
Black Diamond	77 examples	SC-728	0653022 to 0653098
Fruehauf	100 examples	FF-228L	0652710 to 0652784 / 0741464 to 0741488
Kentucky	141 examples		0807970 to 0808110
Omaha	330 examples	F-16	0723547 to 0723846,
			0807665 to 0807694
Reliance	150 examples		0804796 to 0804945
Trailer Co.	100 examples		0653021 to 0653021

A Mystery

Despite great precision in all the administrative documentation about orders and productions, there were a certain number of puzzles which it has been impossible to explain away completely.

For example, in 1943, 100 examples of a 6½-ton Pipe Semitrailer appear in the reception tables for production shared out equally between Fruehauf and Utility (registration numbers included between

On a section of the Red Ball Express, the 3990 QM Truck Co. had the task of convoying tanks of fuel, most of the cartage being made up of Federal tractors and these special semitrailers, August 31, 1944. (U.S. Army SC-198959)

USA-0462584 and USA-0462683). To this day no other administrative source mentions these trailers.

Referring to the title, this designation refers to quite a special tanker trailer. In the photos here tanker ensembles can be seen which are close to the F2A, but with a special form made of vertical flanks, on which hoops could be attached and covered with canvas.

This example of the 6½-ton Pipe Semitrailer showing its flanks and camouflage rollbars. In the background is part of the column that comprised only these special tanker semitrailers; their job was probably filling the jerrycans near the front. (U.S. Army Signal Corps)

5-Ton Truck Tractor Category

This semitrailer tractor category became the preferred cartage for long-distance transport along flat and firm routes. They were 4/5-ton 4x4 Truck Tractors converted to the 4x2 version. Except for one, they were also intended for towing the 6-ton (10-ton Gross) Semitrailer.

There were 16,850 examples of this model delivered by a single company, the International Harvester Company (IHC) with three different models: the KR-11s, the H-542-9, and the H-542-11. Their job, especially the last two, was to ensure that supplies reached the front because there was no rail network from the ports.

A truck from the 349th QM Truck Company (Heavy) which in Europe was part of the Central Europe and Rhineland campaigns. (Signal Corps)

International Harvester KR-11

An atypical vehicle, 1,232 KR-11s were ordered and delivered.

In 1943, the U.S. Army was looking for a tractor designed for the road for its heavy semitrailer. The vehicle did not have a warlike calling; it just did short trips within its big bases located on national soil, resupplying military installations from civilian suppliers and marshaling yards located in the national network. It was not a matter of creating a new truck from scratch, but of using an existing model from the commercial ranges and adapting it by giving it acceptable tires and a satisfactory electrical system, for example.

The choice was made quickly—a model already built for several years by International Harvester Co., which had proved itself to its civilian users. From 1941 when it replaced the DR-70 on the production lines, to 1947 when it was supplanted by the KBR-11, 9,263 examples of the KR-11 had been built, including those supplied to the Army. Considered by its designers as a medium tractor in the civilian 4- to 6-ton administrative class, it became the 5-ton Truck Tractor for the Army.

The International Harvester KR-11 was originally civilian and only required minor modifications to militarize it: specific blackout lighting, removing the right-hand tank and enlarging the left-hand one, standardizing the tires and new paintwork. (IHC)

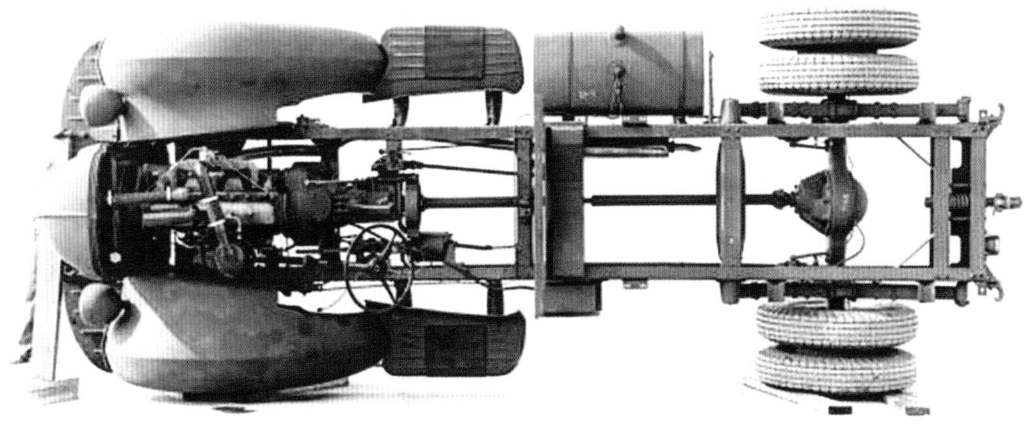

No longer quite civilian, but not quite military either, the prototype has already been given its new rear coupling hook and the front towing hooks. Its running boards and fuel tanks still have to be modified. (IHC)

Right and below: Even when modified, the International Harvester KR-11 cannot disown its civilian origins. (SNL G-542)

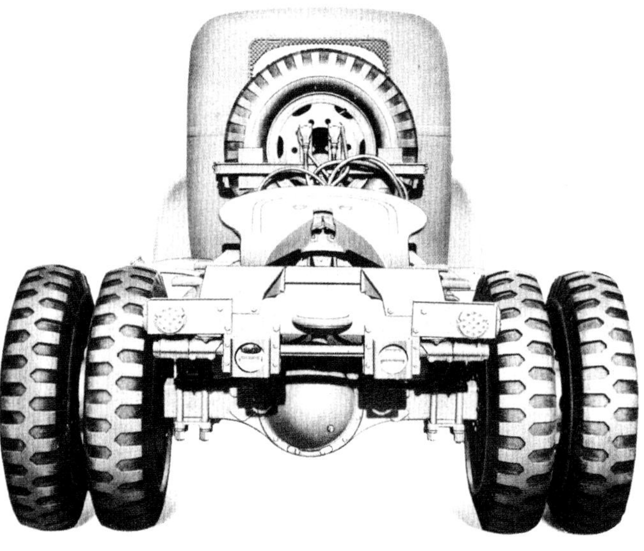

The Shape

The KR-11 was quite a traditional tractor with its cab behind the engine compartment, and with the technical part at the rear on the fifth wheel. Based on a chassis with two main longerons and six crossmembers, this outfit had two differentials and a wheelbase of 161 inches (408.9 cm). Built only with a hardtop cabin, the tractor was 86⅞ inches high (220.66 cm). It was 94⅞ inches (240.98 cm) wide and 239 inches (609.12 cm) long. Its only fuel tank was located on the left-hand side of the chassis; on the right, the spare space on the longeron was taken by a big toolbox. The single spare wheel was located vertically on the back of the cabin.

Weighing in all 9,801 lb (4,449 kg), the KR-11 could tow semitrailers with a maximum weight of 30,000 lb (13,620 kg) but not carry more than 13,000 lb (5,902 kg) on the tractor's fifth wheel. The braking system, working also for the trailers or the haulage, was of the compressed-air type—a Westinghouse Automotive Air Brake System. It was fed by a two-cylinder compressor belt-driven directly from the engine takeoff; the air produced was stocked in the three cylindrical tanks mounted between the chassis longerons. Quick couplers for the trailer brakes were located on the back of the cabin, on the spare wheel cradle.

The Mechanics

Using 10.00x20 12-ply tires, the International Harvester KR-11 rested on two Eaton Manufacturing Co. differentials, a non-motorized I-Beam model for the front and a double reduction model for the rear. The vehicle was powered by an in-house RED-450 gasoline engine in a single block housing six pistons. This ensemble with culverted valves had a capacity of 450.99 cubic inches (7,392 cc), rated at 130 bhp at 2,600 rpm. It was water cooled from a radiator made up of vaned tubes and a water pump located on the front face of the engine block; ventilation was by means of a four-bladed fan to increase the cooling of its 25.5 quarts (2.12 liters) which constituted the cooling circuit.

Transferring the engine drive through a single dry-disk Borg Warner clutch was by means of an IHC gearbox with five forward and one reverse gears. With these mechanics, a Zenith carburetor, an AC pump and a 40-gallon (151-liter) fuel tank, gave the KR-11 a range of between 140.62 (225 km) and 181¼ miles (290 km) and a consumption rate of between 3.51 and 4.53 mpg.

This consumption varied with the type of road, the running conditions, and the configuration—whether towing or not. The high consumption rate was enough for the short missions and distances for which they were intended. All the electrical system worked on 6 volts with a positive earth from two 6-volt batteries arranged in parallel, except for starting the engine which worked with a 12-volt starter. It was thanks to the electrical circuit of the ignition contactor, which alone was fed by the two batteries in series via an electromagnetic contactor, that this differentiation was possible. Most of the electrical parts were made by Delco-Remy.

International Truck Tractor KR-11 Production

Quantity	Orders	Registration Numbers	Comments
30	W-271-ORD-3970	545699 to 5445728	All delivered in 1943
252		546535 to 546786	All delivered in 1944
601	W-271-ORD-11-022-286	571152 to 571752	All delivered in 1944
349		586308 to 586656	128 delivered in 1944 and the other 221 in 1945
Of a total of 1,232 KR-11 Tractors: 30 were delivered in 1943, 981 in 1944, and the last 221 in 1945.			

Registered as USA-571236, this KR-11 was part of a series of 601 vehicles from the second contract. Taking part in a parade in October 1944, it is towing a low-bed-type trailer on which the inflatable element of a floating bridge is presented to the public. The 4th Service Command insignia is on the door. (U.S. Army Signal Corps)

Convoying ammunition, out of a secure bunker, over short distances was one of the missions of the KR-11. The tractor, like the trailer, bears the insignia of the 1st Service Command. (Private Collection)

HC RED 450 ENGINE

Side view of the HC RED-450 engine fitted on the KR-11:

A. Connection to water pump
B. Radiator hose
C. Connection to the radiator
D. Compression line
E. Oil filler
F. Carburetor
G. Filter
H. Coil
I. Coupling hose
J. Air Filter
K. Distributor head
L. Fuel pump
M. Crown fairing
N. Starter
O. Valve
P. Compressor
Q. Support
R. Ground strap
S. Belt
T. Compressor drive pulley
U. Water pump drive pulley
V. Compressor drive belt
W. Fan

Having tried to avoid a disabled civilian vehicle, the driver of this KR-11 took the corner too tightly and couldn't help hitting the verge. Registered USA-545702, this tractor was one of the first series of 30 vehicles from the first supply contract to the Army. It bears the insignia of the 2nd Service Command on its doors. Given the signpost hooked onto the radiator grille, catastrophe has just been avoided—the explosives loaded in the 10-ton Gross Van Semitrailer have remained stable and inert. Collingwood, New Jersey, January 30, 1945. (ACME ref. P-749838)

Coupled to a 7-ton Stake & Platform Cargo Semitrailer whose tailboards have been removed, this KR-11 registered USA-571248 is part of the second contract. The photograph was taken toward the end of the war at Seattle Port of Embarkation (SEPE). (Private Collection)

Hampton Roads Port of Embarkation, Virginia. This is a KR-11 used for towing big vehicles coming off the preparation lines for transport by sea, to be directed toward the trains which transferred them to the quayside. On the door of the tractor is the 3rd Service Command insignia. (U.S. Army Signal Corps)

International Harvester H-542-9/M425

Two road vehicles saw the light of day at the same time, one named "Light Duty" and the other "Heavy Duty." They were however of a very similar design and only a few details allowed them to be differentiated.

There were 4,640 examples of the first tractor, the "Light Duty," delivered under the manufacturer's designation of H-542-9 and the Army's M-425. In the IHC's nomenclature, the H designated Harvester, the 5 for 5 ton, the 42 for 4x2, and the 9 to recall the size of the tires which were 9.00x20.

As soon as the invasion plans of Europe were made, plans were also made for resupplying the continent which gave rise from August 1944 onward to the famous routes of the Red Ball Express and the ABC Route in Northwestern Europe.

Specific needs for vehicles travelling long distances also arose from this logistical concept. There were two conclusions: the existing pool of tractors with a forward cabin was not adapted to long distances because they were too heavy, with a high fuel consumption rate; and there was no alternative 4x2 version which was enough for the carriageways.

The new project took shape under the Ordnance Department's management, and International Harvesters designed two prototypes on a similar basis but with different capabilities for the two ranges of specific uses. The first was intended for towing semitrailers theoretically classified as 16-foot/5-ton and the second for the 25-foot/10-ton semitrailers.

From this moment onward, it was understood that these new vehicles could easily be made by other companies and that the orders would be shared.

Top: Putting this M425 through extreme conditions on the factory's test track. It's at the limit of stalling with the 5-ton S&P Semitrailer for which it was designed. It was to avoid this that the M426 would have its fifth wheel raised by a few inches compared with the chassis. (International Harvester)

Center: Two quite visible aspects of the M425: the searchlight mounted on a bracket and the fifth wheel positioned directly on the chassis longerons. The tanks are the early models with the forward filling nozzle, thus two versions, the right and the left, so as to remain symmetrical. (International Harvester)

Bottom: The standardization of the fuel tanks with a central filling nozzle made spare part management easier—no need for two different models. (Private Collection)

Differentiation

Visually it was difficult to distinguish the light from the heavy versions, but technically there were certain particularities.

They were fitted with 9.00x20 10-ply with a pressure of 65 psi, 11 leaf springs on each differential plus eight extra ones on the rear, a double electric two-tone vibration horn and an auxiliary horn operated from the dashboard, and there was a searchlight on the left of the cabin.

M425 & M426 TRUCK PRODUCTION

5-Ton 4x2 Light Duty H-542-9/M45 Truck Tractors

Quantity	Orders	Registration Numbers	Comments
1,818	W-271-ORD-4846	559288 to 561105	All delivered in 1944 (International Harvester M425)
2,640		583258 to 585897	2,212 delivered in 1944 and 428 in 1945 (International Harvester M425)
182		586126 to 586307	All delivered in 1945 (International Harvester M425)
1,197	W-33-008-ORD-2145	-	M425 became M426 in 1945, modified by Marmon-Herrington
3			Became 10-ton 6x4 in 1945 modified by Marmon-Herrington
Of a total of 4,640 M425 Truck Tractors: 4,030 were delivered in 1944 and 610 in 1945.			

5-Ton 4x2 Heavy Duty H-542-9/M426 Truck Tractors

Quantity	Orders	Registration Numbers	Comments
3,500	W-271-ORD-4846	555288 to 558787	All delivered in 1944 (International M426)
2,950		580308 to 583257	1,350 delivered in 1944 and 1,600 in 1945 (International M426)
228		585898 to 586125	All delivered in 1945. (International M426)
1,100	W-04-200-ORD-113	5106841 to 5107940	750 delivered in 1944 and 350 in 1945 (Kenworth M426)
2,990	W-33-008-ORD-1638	5108051 to 5111040	2,000 delivered in 1944 and 990 in 1945 (Marmon-Herrington M426)
10		5129753 to 5129762	All delivered in 1945 (Marmon-Herrington M426)
200		5133792 to 5133991	All delivered in 1945 (Marmon-Herrington M426)
Of a total of 10,978 M426 Truck Tractors: 7,600 were delivered in 1944 and 3,378 in 1945.			

The first 622 M425s received fuel tanks with a filler centered toward the front (one for the left and another for the right); the rest of the production had symmetrical tanks with the filler centered along the length. But most importantly was the positioning of the fifth wheel: it was fixed directly

Anything to encourage Americans to subscribe to war loans was interesting, even showing captured materiel. At Newark, New Jersey, this M425 is towing a 12½-ton C-2 Wrecking Type Semitrailer carrying a German V-1 flying bomb. (Private Collection)

Above: Even if these 5-ton 4x2 trucks were intended for the supply routes through France and Belgium, they were nonetheless present in small numbers in other theaters, like here in Italy, in the 37th QM Battalion of the Peninsula Base Section (PBS). (U.S. Army SC-198299)

Below: The big supply routes like the ABC Route in Belgium (pictured) were crucial to logistics in the second half of 1944 and early 1945. Without them, the war would have lasted several months longer. The 5-ton International Harvester Truck Tractors were the centerpiece of this success. (U.S. Army Signal Corps)

on the chassis longerons, and its axis was located 3 inches (7.62 cm) in front of the longitudinal axis of the rear differential.

All the H-542-9s were built by IHC and were given a chassis number between H-542-9-001 and H-542-9-4640. In 1945, Marmon-Herrington received an order to modify 1,200 examples to the standards of the heavy version of the 5-ton 4x2 truck; only 1,197 of them were modified, the remaining three were transformed into 6x6 10-ton Cargo Trucks.

The Shape

The International H-542-0 was a COE-type semitrailer tractor with a technical part on the rear fifth wheel. Based on a chassis with two main longerons and six crossmembers, this outfit had two differentials and a wheelbase of 156 inches (297.18 cm). Built only with a soft-top cabin, the tractor was 102½ inches high (260.35 cm) in its hooded configuration; the bare cabin enabled it to gain some 19 inches (about 50 cm) for sea transport. It was 94½ inches (240.67 cm) wide and 200 inches (508 cm) long.

Weighing 11,400 lb net (5,176 kg), the M425 could tow semitrailers with a maximum weight of 16,000 lb (7,264 kg) but not take more than 7,850 lb (3,564

kg) on the tractor's fifth wheel. The braking system, working also for the trailers or the haulage, was of the Westinghouse Automotive Air Brake System compressed-air type. It was fed by a two-cylinder compressor located on the left-hand side of the engine block and was driven by a belt; the air produced was stocked in the two cylindrical tanks in the chassis just behind the fuel tanks. Quick-fitting couplings for the trailer brakes were located directly behind the cabin.

The Mechanics

Using 9.00x20 10-ply tires, the M425 rested on a free front differential of the I-Beam type made by Timken-Detroit, a 26450-WX3 not motorized at the front, and an R-3100WX5 double reduction type at the rear. The vehicle was powered by a RED-450-D International turbo-charged gasoline engine in a single block housing six pistons. This ensemble had a capacity of 455.99 cubic inches (4,474 cc), rated at 124½ bhp at 2,600 rpm. It was water cooled from a radiator made up of vaned tubes and a water pump located on the front of the engine block, ventilation being by means of a four-bladed fan to increase the cooling of its 36 quarts (34.06 liters) which made up the cooling circuit.

Transferring the engine drive through a single dry-disk W.C. Lippe clutch was by means of an International F54D gearbox with five forward and one reverse gears. With a Zenith carburetor, an AC pump and a 2 x 40-gallon (302.80-liter) reserve of fuel, it had a range of between 320 miles (515 km) by itself and 240 miles (390 km) coupled with a maximum payload, which was allowed, or an average fuel consumption of between 3 and 4 mpg, this consumption varying with the type of road, the running conditions, and the configuration—whether towing or not. The whole electrical setup worked on a 6-volt system from a single 6-volt battery, most of the electrical parts being made by Delco-Remy.

From top to bottom:

Not especially intended for being transported by air, this M425 is going to be entirely dismantled so it can be transferred to China. The horns are quite visible, above the standard military model and below the double horn of the vibration hooter. India, November 3, 1944. (U.S. Army SC-269463)

Entirely dismantled into subassemblies, it was only in this form that it could be loaded into the fuselage of its transporter. (U.S. Army SC-269464)

Ready to leave China-wards via the airlift, Nohanbari Airfield, Assam Province, India. The various elements are resting on the Air Force's M5 bomb carrier trailers. (U.S. Army SC-269598)

The transformation of three M425s into 10-ton 6x4 M426 Cargo Trucks by Marmon-Herrington in 1945 was spectacular. Except for the cabin, there was no difference from the original vehicle. (U.S. Army Signal Corps)

International Harvester H-542-11/M426

10,978 examples of the second model, called "Heavy Duty," were delivered as the factory designation H-542-11 and for the Army as the M426, the H for Harvester, the 5 for 5-ton, the 42 for the 4x2 and the 11 for the tire size which was 11.00x20.

Compared with the M425, the M426 no longer had its searchlight or the second horn; its particularities were 11.00x20 12-ply tires with 50 psi at the front and 70 psi at the rear; there were 13 leaf springs on the front differential and 16 leaf assemblies on the rear, plus 10 auxiliary ones. As far as the axle and the fifth wheel coupling were concerned, they were moved 6 inches (15.24 cm) in relation to the differential axis, which was separated from the chassis longerons by an intermediate frame.

Above: Coupled to the 10-ton S&P Semitrailer, the M426 was imposing. Despite its registration number USA-5110842 which made it a Marmon-Herrington production, the general shape of the truck tractor remains the one designed by International Harvester. (U.S. Army Signal Corps)

Below: This view reveals the fifth wheel and the spacer system which raised it above the chassis. (U.S. Army Signal Corps)

This extra height avoided difficulties when the truck was negotiating rough ground. The bigger tires changed certain dimensions of the vehicle compared with the light version. The wheelbase was lengthened by 3 inches, and the width and the height were also slightly increased as well as the weight and certain performances.

There were 11,500 examples ordered from six companies: 4,000 from International Harvester, 1,200 from Kenworth, 3,000 from Marmon-Herrington, 400 from Ward LaFrance, 400 from Corbitt, and 2,500 from White.

But as often happened, the orders were considerably modified, and the purchases from Ward LaFrance, Corbitt and White were not finalized, the shared orders and production was stopped after 10,978 trucks had been made. International Harvester built 6,678 of which the first 1,214 had the filling pipe offset forward; Kenworth built 1,100 examples all with the filling nozzles centered, and Marmon-Herrington 3,200 with only the first six fitted with a forward filling nozzle.

The Shape

The International Harvester was a COE-type truck with a technical part on the rear fifth wheel. Based on a chassis with two main longerons and

Top: This M426 has been made by Kenworth, one of the 1,100 examples ordered from this firm. (U.S. Army Signal Corps)

Above: The end of the production line at Marmon-Herrington and the final inspections before delivery. The increase in tire diameter meant the spare wheel protruded from the side of the cabin, one of the particularities of the M426 compared to the M425. (Marmon-Herrington)

Left: Chained and strapped on a railway flatbed, these M426s are ready for the Ordnance Department depots, to be finished off by being fitted with the spare wheels for example. (Marmon-Herrington)

six crossmembers, this outfit rested on two differentials with a wheelbase of 120 inches (304.8 cm).

Built only with a soft-top cabin, the tractor was 104¾ inches high (266.07 cm) in its canvas cabin configuration; the topless version enabled it to gain some 19 inches (about 50 cm) during sea transport. It was 97½ inches (247.65 cm) wide and 200 inches (508 cm) long.

Weighing in all 12,100 lb (5,493 kg), the M426 could tow semitrailers with a maximum weight of 40,000 lb (18,160 kg) but not take more than 13,000 lb (5,902 kg) on the tractor's fifth wheel. The braking system, working also for the trailers or the haulage, was of the Westinghouse Automotive Air Brake System compressed-air type. It was fed by a two-cylinder compressor located on the left-hand side of the engine block and was driven by a belt; the air produced was stocked in the two cylindrical tanks within the chassis just behind the fuel tanks. Quick-fitting couplings for the trailer brakes were located directly behind the cabin.

The Mechanics

Apart from the 11.00x20 tires, the differentials and the powerplant were identical to those of the M425, like the gearbox and the fuel consumption.

Top: On the ABC Route, winter 1944/45. With the name of *Angelina*, the 10-ton semitrailer of this M426 is fitted with its canvas hood. This rare configuration leads one to think that its load was more precious than the others, most certainly cartons of rations. (U.S. Army Signal Corps)

Above: Spring 1945, the weather conditions have calmed down and the multitude of convoys can resume undiminished. Here, the 3573rd QM Truck Company on the main road linking Tirlemont to Liège in Belgium. (U.S. Army Signal Corps)

Right: November 11, 1944, en route for Paris, a convoy consisting of M426s and 6-ton Refrigerator Semitrailers of the 626th QM Refrigeration Company, transporting frozen turkeys for Thanksgiving. (U.S. Army Signal Corps)

Top: On the Red Ball Express routes, the H-542-11 International Harvester is towing a 10-ton S&P semitrailer considerably modified by getting rid of most of the height on its sides. The four vats contain fuel. This configuration was a specialty of the 3580th Quartermaster Truck Company which converted several semitrailers in this way. (U.S. Army Signal Corps)

Middle: Germany, 1945, a rest and regrouping zone for this transport company. If we refer to the registration numbers, it appears that the first vehicles are Marmon-Herringtons, although the second bears the registration number of Fire Trucks with the first two numbers being 50. A mistake in the field or in the factory? (U.S. Army Signal Corps)

Bottom left: France, November 29, 1944, T/Sgt John Gietl at the wheel of his M426 towing a 6-ton Refrigerator Semitrailer, of the 485th QM Refrigeration Company. On the double door giving access to the machinery, an evocative slogan. (U.S. Army SC-197335)

Bottom right: The small community of Sissone near Laon, in the Aisne Department, hosted Camp Washington in 1945. This redeployment center was one of the stages for transferring materiel from Europe to the Pacific. The vehicles were inspected and reconditioned (summarily) for use on the other side of the globe. This is the case for these 5-ton 4x2 Truck Tractors in June 1945. (U.S. Army Signal Corps)

10-Ton (14-Ton Gross) Stake & Platform Semitrailer

With 18,938 examples delivered, this semitrailer was the most built of all, by 17 different manufacturers. Built only in 1944 and 1945, it began life at the same time as the Harvester M426. Also called Cargo by analogy, they were intended for transporting general supplies. Made up of a platform with removable drop-sides, it allowed for various configurations

These trailers with single axles and with twin 11.00x20 14-ply wheels had a wheelbase of 226 inches (574.04 cm)—axle differential to the coupling point—and a total length of 306½ inches (778.51 cm), a width of 96 inches (243.84 cm), and a height of 95 inches (241.3 cm). Weighing 9,438 lb (4,281 kg) empty, they could take a maximum weight of 20,017 lb (9,080kg). The distribution of the mass had the tractor's fifth wheel take, fully loaded, 12,531 lb (5,684 kg) and 16,924 lb (7,677 kg) on its axle, a weight distribution ratio of 42% to 58%.

Top: Without its drop-sides, the 10-ton S&P became a loading platform for voluminous packages. This example is being towed by a White 444, registration number USA-4835153. (U.S. Army Signal Corps)

Middle: A rare configuration for this 10-ton S&P fitted with a canvas hood mounted on its arches. It was one of the 18,938 examples delivered to the Army.

Left: The front and rear sides of the same trailer. Its registration number is not visible, but it was assigned to the 349th QM Truck Company. (U.S. Army Signal Corps)

Above: Loaded with combat rations and waiting to be transferred from England to France, these 10-ton S&P semitrailers present two versions of the drop-sides, both full and slatted. (U.S. Army Signal Corps)

10-Ton Stake & Platform Semitrailer Production

Manufacturer	Quantity	Model	Registration Numbers
American Body	984 examples	1025	0740747 to 0741046 / 0749566 to 0749865 / 0912166 to 0912549
Carter	600 examples	1025	0726047 to 0726646
Coleman	720 examples	1025	0801134 to 0801853
Doersey	1,630 examples	SKD2361	0727847 to 0728646 / 0752266 to 0752465 / 0908766 to 0909395
Highway	2,000 examples	SKD2361	0736647 to 0738646
Keystone	784 examples	SKD2361	0750766 to 0751165 / 0912550 to 0912933
Krieger	1,841 examples	SKD2361	0754374 to 0755573 / 0911068 to 0911708
Miller	1,890 examples	SKD2361	0752466 to 0753765 / 0909396 to 0909985
Pike	480 examples	1025	0758378 to 0758857 / 0758378 to 0758657
Omaha	461 examples	10255	0751966 to 0752265 / 0910902 to 0911062
Oneida	600 examples	SKD2361	0753774 to 0754373
Quenn City	1,876 examples	1025	0755574 to 0756573 / 0910026 to 0910901
Springfield	1,188 examples	1025	0751166 to 0751965 / 0912934 to 0913321
Strick	1,240 examples	SKD2361	0757574 to 0758373 / 0911726 to 0912165
Timpte	1,044 examples	SKD2361	0740447 to 0740746 / 0749866 to 0750165 / 0913322 to 0913705 / 0928907 to 0928966
Trailmobile	1,000 examples	1025	0756574 to 0757573
Winter-Weiss	600 examples	1025	0750166 to 0750765

Right: Waiting for a railway bridge to be rebuilt across the Rhine, the contents of the wagons are transferred to 10-ton S&Ps from the 3629th QM Truck Company, tasked with convoying it via a pontoon bridge to supply the Seventh U.S. Army, Ludwigshafen, Germany. (U.S. Army SC-227312)

5

5/6-Ton Truck Tractor Category

This category of semitrailer tractors is quite special because the tractors were intended for the Corps of Engineers specifically to transport bridge components equipping the unit at the beginning of the 1940s.

There were 3,411 5/6-ton 4x4 Truck Tractors delivered by two companies, the Autocar Company and the Mack Manufacturing Co. of New York. Two vehicle models were concerned, the Autocar U-8144-T and the Mack NJU1/2.

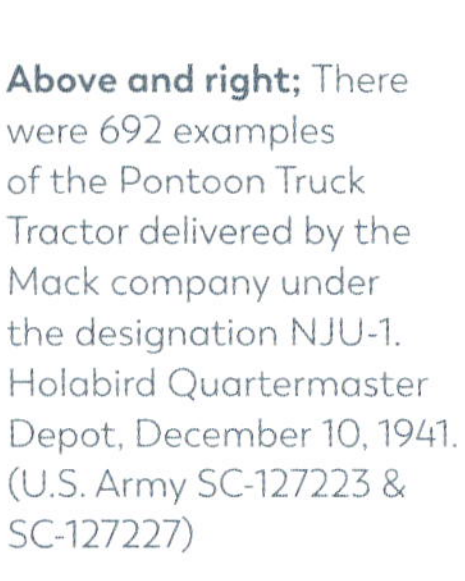

Above and right; There were 692 examples of the Pontoon Truck Tractor delivered by the Mack company under the designation NJU-1. Holabird Quartermaster Depot, December 10, 1941. (U.S. Army SC-127223 & SC-127227)

Mack NJU-1 & NJU-2

To respond to demand, the U.S. Army counted on the Corps of Engineers which had the educated specialists and a great variety of materiel at its disposal. Among these were the pontoons, including heavy, cumbersome elements which were transported with the help of special semitrailers.

The first of these vehicles was the 5/6-ton 4x4 NJU-1 Pontoon Truck Tractor built by the Mack Manufacturing Corporation. 14 examples of the Mack truck equipped the Heavy Pontoon Battalions of which 15 were deployed during the war.

Mack Manufacturing Corporation NJU-1 & NJU-2 Truck Production			
Quantity	Orders	Registration Numbers	Comments
1	W-271-ORD-3970	51761	All delivered in 1941
547		51763 to 52309	All delivered in 1941
8		52490 to 52497	All delivered in 1941 (NJU-2)
111		52310 to 52420	All delivered in 1941
33		52457 to 52489	6 delivered in 1941 and 27 in 1942
Of a total of 692 Pontoon Truck Tractor NJU-1s and eight Truck Tractor NJU-2s: 673 were delivered in 1941, the last 27 in 1942.			

There was a long history between Mack and the U.S. Army, a fruitful collaboration when it was a question of supplying heavy-tonnage vehicles. It was therefore not unusual for the firm to receive the order W-398-QM-8977 in 1941 for 804 vehicles—104 6-ton 6x6 NM3 Cargo Trucks and 700 5/6-ton 4x4 NJU Truck Tractors. 692 were NJU-1 Pontoons and the other eight were NJU-2s. With a lightened front suspension and without the storage chest, the latter was intended for towing heavy topographical trailers.

The Shape

The Mack NJU-1 was a COE semitrailer tractor and a technical part with a large storage chest plus a fifth wheel on the rear. Based on a chassis with two main longerons and five crossmembers, this outfit had two differentials with a wheelbase of 148 inches (375.92 cm).

Built only with a hardtop cabin, the tractor was 114 inches (289.56 cm) high, 92½ inches (243.84 cm) wide, and 237 inches (601.98 cm) long. Its single fuel tank was located on the left-hand side of the chassis; on the right, the empty space on the longeron was taken by a large tool and battery chest. The spare wheel was positioned vertically on the back of the pontonier's chest.

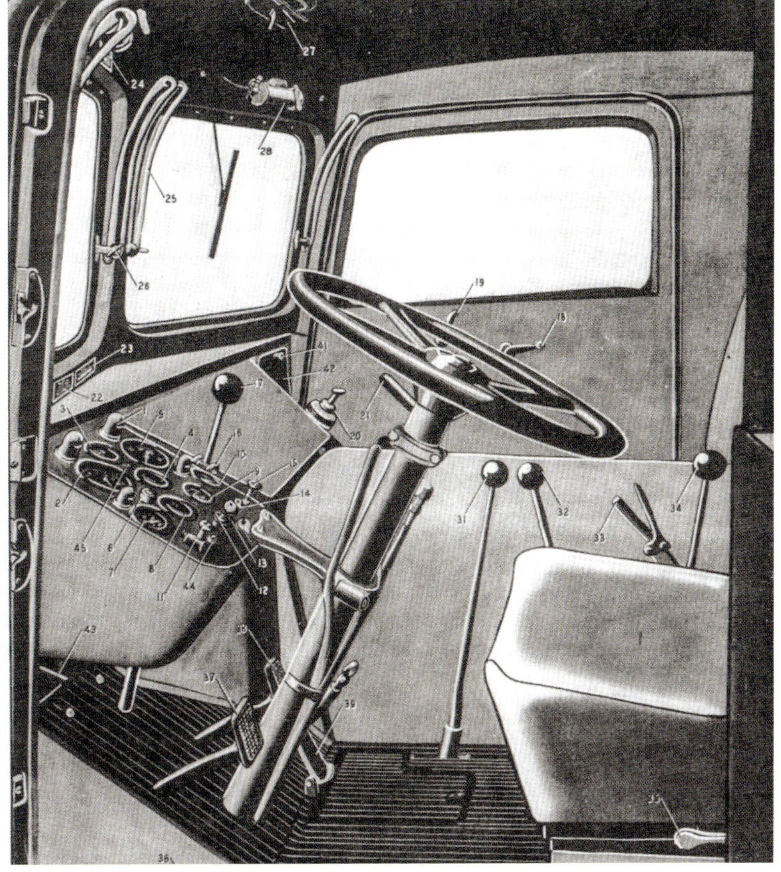

Unlike most military vehicles, the NJUs had no dashboard but rather a console containing all the control instruments. (Sourced TM 10-1705)

Below: March 1942, Fort Benning, the 87th Engineer Heavy Pontoon Battalion has finished loading its materiel on wagons for the spring maneuvers. (U.S. Army SC-133295)

Weighing in all 16,850 lb (7,527 kg), the NJU-1 could tow semitrailers with a maximum weight of 30,000 lb (13,620 kg) but not take more than 10,460 lb (4,748 kg) on the tractor's fifth wheel. The braking system of the tractor, working also for the trailer, was of the Westinghouse Automotive Air Brake System compressed-air type. It was fed by a two-cylinder compressor driven directly by the engine, the air produced being stocked in the two cylindrical tanks installed on the outside of the chassis longerons, just in front of the rear wheels. Quick-fitting couplings for the trailer brakes were located directly behind the big accessories chest.

The Mechanics

Using 12.00x20 14-ply tires, the Mack NJU-1 rested on an F-3100-W-X-5 Timken-Detroit differential at the front and a WIS-R-3100 Wisconsin differential at the rear, both being of the double reduction type. The vehicle was powered by an EN-532 Mack gasoline engine in a single block housing six pistons. This ensemble had a capacity of 532 cubic inches (8,720 cc), rated at 136 bhp at 2,400 rpm. It was water cooled by a radiator made up of vaned tubes and a water pump located on the front of the engine block, ventilation being by means of a four-bladed fan to increase the cooling of its 40 quarts (37.84 liters), constituting the cooling circuit. Transferring the engine drive through a single dry-disk W.C. Lippe clutch was by means of a TR-32 Timken-Detroit gearbox with five forward and one reverse gears, and a T-76 Timken-Detroit two-stage transfer box which was also used to engage the front differential, transforming a 4x2 into a 4x4.

Below: NJU-1 Pontoon Truck Tractor and 25-ton Pontoon Semitrailer with a mixed load, 17th Engineer Battalion. (U.S. Army SC-133295)

There does not seem to be any logic to the way barges are loaded on the 25-ton Pontoon Semitrailer. 87th Heavy Pontoon Battalion at Fort Benning in March 1942. (U.S. Army Signal Corps)

With these mechanics, a Stromberg carburetor, an AC pump, and a 60-gallon (227.10-liter) fuel tank, the Mack NJU-1 had an average range of 342 miles (550.28 km), or an average consumption rate of 5.7 mpg, this consumption varying with the type of road, the running conditions, and the configuration—whether towing or not. All the electrical system of the truck worked on 6 volts with a positive earth from two 6-volt batteries arranged in parallel, except for starting the engine which worked with a 12-volt starter. It was thanks to the ignition contactor's electrical circuit, which alone was fed by the two batteries in series via an electromagnetic contactor, that this differentiation was possible. Most of the electrical parts were made by Delco-Remy.

Supplied by Gar Wood as the 3U615 with a capacity of 15,000 lb (6,810 kg), the winch was powered by the engine. The engine power was transmitted via a cross-link gimbal through a power takeoff located on the left-hand side of the gear box. The system was engaged by a lever situated like all the main controls between the driver's and the conveyer's seat. Like most of the vehicles bought before 1943, all the NJUs had a closed-in cabin derived directly from the civilian Mack productions, while the big chest was made by the Galion company and weighed 1,060 lb (481 kg) alone.

Top left The Mack NJU-1 was one of the most compact semitrailer tractors. Its front winch was barely visible, and the fender hardly protruded compared with the radiator grille. (U.S. Army Signal Corps)

Left: The winch was housed under the vehicle, beneath the radiator and protected by two big flat spring leaves. (U.S. Army SC-133284)

Below: Because of the quantity and the length of the vehicles, the Heavy Pontoon Battalions were big units to move around, usually constituting a column almost 3 kilometers long. (U.S. Army SC-119903)

Left: The Heavy Pontoon Battalions trained for almost three years in setting up pontoon bridges. Most of them were equipped overseas with the Autocar U-8144-T version. But a few units equipped with NJU-Ts went right up to the gates of Berlin. (U.S. Army SC-124355)

Right: Photos showing NJU-1s in Europe are rare. Recognizable at the rear of the photograph by its two dorsal windows, these three brand-new Macks have been stocked in the G-45 Supply Depot at Thatcham, England, April 8, 1944. (U.S. Army SC-189366)

Left: Bowling Green, Ohio, December 1942, the Daybrook Hydraulic Corporation is testing a gantry for launching and recovering Marine Corps assault barges. The NJU-1 is fitted with balloon-type tires for better traction on soft ground. (Private Collection)

Autocar U-8144-T

With 2,711 examples delivered, the Autocar U-8144-T was the most ordered model of Pontoon Truck Tractor. It was not very different from the Mack NJU-1 in shape and purpose.

Both were intended for the same sorts of jobs, but they didn't work together because their mechanics were different. As well as the pontoon truck tractors, the base and mechanics were produced in three versions: a prototype with a skip, a second equipped with a crane, and 604 trucks with a technical platform without winch which were given the designation U-8144 Van Truck, having lost the suffix T.

The Shape

The U-8144-T Autocar was a COE-type semitrailer tractor and a technical part with a big chest plus a fifth wheel on the rear. Built on a chassis with two main longerons and five crossmembers, this outfit had two differentials, with a wheelbase of 163½ inches (415.29 cm). Built with a hardtop cabin for the first 1,431 examples then a soft top for the

Left: On August 11, 1941, the Autocar Co. delivered the pre-series model of its U-8144-T to the Aberdeen Proving Ground. At the time there was only one fuel tank. The second fuel tank was not installed until mid-production. (Autocar Co.)

Below: Behind the cabin the big chest whose sides open downward, gave access to the bridging equipment and tackle, which were stored there for transport. (Autocar Co.)

following examples, the tractor was 111 inches high (281.94 cm) in its closed cabin configuration; the soft-top version enabled it to gain some 19 inches (about 50 cm) for sea transport. It was 98¹/₈ inches (249.24 cm) wide and 296¾ inches (753.74 cm) long.

At first, a single 60-gallon (227.1-liter) fuel tank was installed on the outside of the longeron, just in front of the rear wheels. In the mid-production, a second reserve 30-gallon (113.55-liter) tank was fitted. On the right-hand side, the spare space on the longeron was occupied by a large tool and battery chest. The spare wheel was located vertically on the back of the pontonier's chest.

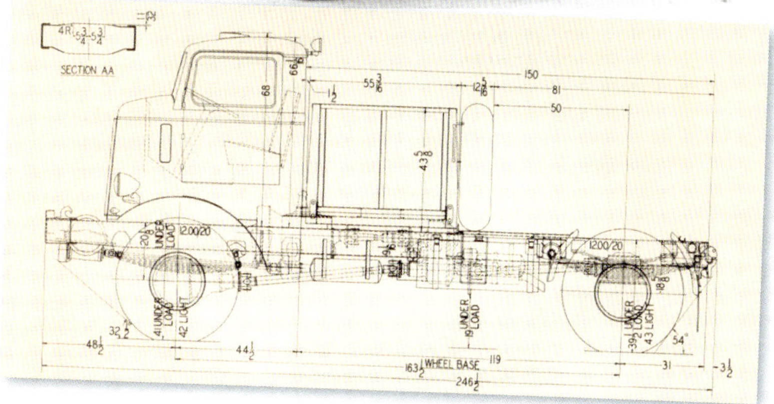

With a net weight of 16,600 lb (7,536 kg), the U-8144-T could tow semitrailers with a maximum weight of 30,000 lb (13,620 kg) but not take more

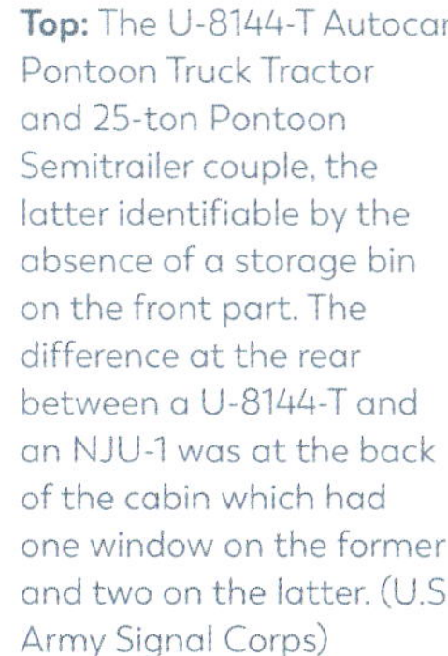

Top: The U-8144-T Autocar Pontoon Truck Tractor and 25-ton Pontoon Semitrailer couple, the latter identifiable by the absence of a storage bin on the front part. The difference at the rear between a U-8144-T and an NJU-1 was at the back of the cabin which had one window on the former and two on the latter. (U.S. Army Signal Corps)

Above: Fully illustrated, the February 1942 TM-10-1119 technical manual provides all the truck's dimensions.

Left: The first 1,431 trucks delivered had a hardtop cabin. (U.S. Army Signal Corps)

INSTRUMENTS & CONTROLS

1) Name plate
2) Transmission and Transfer Case Diagram Plate
3) Winch Plate
4) Drain Caution Plate
5) Publication Reference Plate
6) Engine Speed Caution Plate
7) Buzzer Caution Plate (Brakes)
8) Winch Lever
9) Transfer Case Gear Shift Lever
10) Front Axle Declutching Lever
11) Main Transmission Gear Shift Lever
12) Hand Brake Lever
13) Clutch Operating Pedal
14) Foot Brake Pedal
15) Starter Button
16) Foot Dimmer Switch
17) Viscometer
18) Ammeter
19) Auxiliary Ammeter
20) Air Pressure Gauge
21) Tachometer
22) Speedometer
23) Oil Pressure Gauge
24) Heat Indicator Gauge
25) Gasoline Gauge
26) Windshield Wiper Control Valve
27) 4-Position Light Switch
28) Carburetor Choke
29) Tachometer Lock Switch
30) Ignition Switch
31) Throttle Button
32) Panel Lights Rheostat
33) Air Brake Hand Control Valve
34) Horn Button
35) Rear View Mirror
36) Door Opening Handle
37) Door Window Regulator Lever
38) Searchlight Control Button

Opposite: 25-ton Pontoon Semitrailer with only one barge. Fort Leonard Wood, Missouri, January 1942. (U.S. Army Signal Corps)

than 10,700 lb (4,858 kg) on the fifth wheel of the tractor. The braking system, working also for the trailers or the haulage, was of the Westinghouse Automotive Air Brake System compressed-air type. It was fed by a two-cylinder compressor driven directly by the engine; the air produced was stocked in the two cylindrical tanks, one inside the chassis on the left-hand side longeron, just behind the cabin and one outside the right-hand side longeron in front of the twin rear wheels. Quick-fit couplings for the trailer brakes were located directly behind the cabin.

The Mechanics

Using 12.00x20 14-ply tires, the U-8144-T rested on two differentials, an F-3100-W Timken-Detroit for the front and an R-3100-W for the rear, both being of the double reduction type. The vehicle was powered by a Model RXC Hercules gasoline engine in a single block housing six pistons. This ensemble had a capacity of 529 cubic inches (8,700 cc), rated at 131 bhp at 2,300 rpm. It was water cooled by a radiator made up of vaned tubes and a water pump located on the front of the engine block, ventilation being by means of a six-bladed fan to increase the cooling of its 40 quarts (37.84 liters) which constituted the cooling circuit.

Above: The USA-53169, a vehicle from the very first generation, had a spectacular career end. Its hardtop cabin was cut off and it became the prototype for the soft-top version. It was also given a canvas door and a second fuel tank. Finally, the cabin was given metal half-doors, and the two tanks were swapped. (U.S. Army Signal Corps)

Below: September 1944, the 1303rd Engineer Battalion has thrown a Bailey bridge across the Saône at Chalon, France. The U-8144-T crossing it belongs to the 88th Heavy Pontoon Battalion attached to the Third U.S. Army (U.S. Army SC-232769)

Transferring the engine drive through a single dry-disk W.C. Lippe clutch was by means of a TR-32 Timken-Detroit gearbox with five forward and one reverse gears, and a T-76 Timken-Detroit two-stage transfer box which was also used to engage the front differential, transforming a 4x2 into a 4x4. With these mechanics, a Zenith carburetor, an AC pump, and a 90-gallon (340.65-liter) fuel tank in its later version, gave the U-8144-T a range of between 477 miles (767.49 km) and a consumption rate of 5.3 mpg, this consumption varying with the type of road, the running conditions, and the configuration—whether towing or not.

U-8144-T & U-8144 Autocar Co. Truck Production

Quantity	Orders	Registration Numbers	Comments
160	W-398-QM-10325	52930 to 53089	52 delivered in 1941 and 108 in 1942
80		53117 to 53196	All delivered in 1942
142	W-398-QM-DA-7	none	40 delivered in 1941 and 102 in 1942
72	W-398-QM-DA-526	534478 to 534549	24 delivered in 1942 and 48 in 1943
45	W-398-QM-10803	53526 to 53570	All delivered in 1942
1	W-398-QM-11562	55274	Delivered in 1942 (Dump Truck)
828	W-670-ORD-3178	55953 to 57322	187 delivered in 1942, 532 in 1943 and 109 in 1944
542			286 delivered in 1942 and 256 in 1943 (Truck Van w/o winch)
1	W-670-ORD-3354	0032253	Delivered in 1942 (Experimental Truck Tractor with a crane)
654	W-670-ORD-3355	541581 to 542234	399 delivered in 1943 and 255 in 1944
166		553473 to 553638	All delivered in 1944
272	W-670-ORD-36-034-372	590430 to 590701	All delivered in 1944
65	W-670-ORD-36-034-1789	5117097 to 5117161	All delivered in 1944 (Truck Van w/o winch)
292	W-670-ORD-36-034-2500	5122489 to 5122683	All delivered in 1945
Of a total of 2,711 Pontoon Truck Tractor U-8144-Ts and 607 Van-Truck U-8144s + 1 Crane Truck and one Dump Truck: 92 were delivered in 1941, 834 in 1942, 1,235 in 1943, 785 in 1944, and the last 374 in 1945.			

An impressive convoy on Belgian roads, early 1945, heading for the Rhine. The tractors belong to the 52nd Heavy Pontoon Battalion. (Associated Press)

All the electrics worked on a 6-volt system from two 6-volt batteries arranged in parallel, except for starting the engine which worked with a 12-volt starter. It was thanks to the electrical circuit of the ignition contactor, which alone was fed by the two batteries in series via an electromagnetic contactor, that this differentiation was possible. Most of the electrical parts were made by Delco-Remy.

The Gar Wood winch was identical to that of the Mack truck.

If we do not consider the 214 U-8144-T tractors delivered in the context of the Defense Aid program and whose destination was not stated, we are left with 133 examples which were delivered under the cover of the Lend-Lease, nine for the UK and 124 for the French forces.

An impressive convoy which, in gloomy weather—a circumstantial ally given the need to keep the operation secret—moves inexorably toward Germany. (Keystone Photo ref. 485568)

Semitrailers Specific to 5/6-Ton 4x4 Tractors

The Pontoon Truck Tractors were given two special trailers for transporting parts and barges for making the pontoon bridges.

The two trucks we have just studied and the types of trailers were used with rigid floats before the inflatable floats were introduced. The two semitrailers had almost the same technical features and differed only in the load they could carry. Other semitrailers, a restricted number of them and always for the Engineers' use, were associated to the 5/6-ton Truck Tractors.

The 10-Ton Pontoon Semitrailer

Built by the Fruehauf Trailer Company and the Trailer Company of America, this first trailer was mainly planned for transporting parts of the 10-ton floating bridge. It had a total length of 375¼ inches (953.14 cm), a width of 96 inches (243.84 cm), and a height of 80 inches (203.2 cm). They weighed 7,200 lb (3,269 kg) empty and could take a maximum weight of 18,000 lb (8,172 kg). The distribution of the mass had the tractor's fifth wheel take 10,900 lb (4,949 kg) and 14,300 lb (6,492 kg) on its only axle with 12.00x20 14-ply tires, a weight distribution ratio of 43% to 57%.

Its main feature was the big stowage chest above its gooseneck. It was an early example and only 400

A U-8144-T Autocar Pontoon Truck Tractor and a 10-ton Pontoon Semitrailer coupling. This semitrailer is identifiable by the stowage chest located on the front part. All metal in the early versions, it was later made of wood. (U.S. Army Signal Corps)

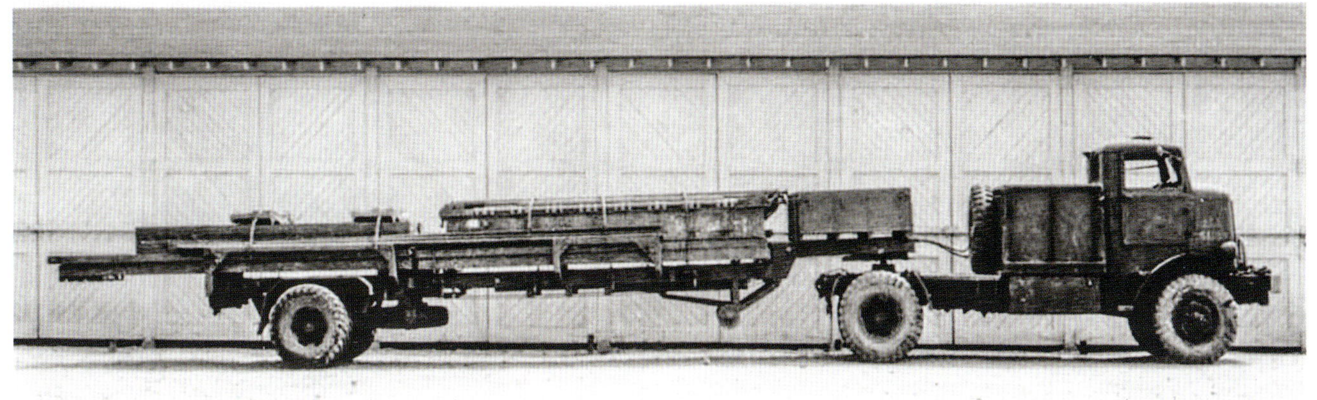

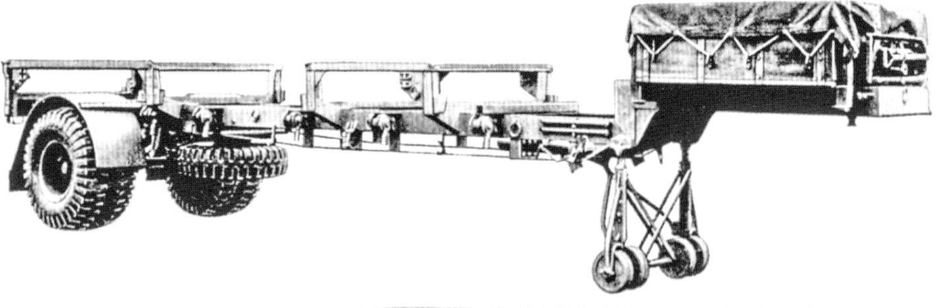

Left and below: The 10-ton Pontoon Semitrailer was an ensemble of separate frames which enabled various lengthy items to be loaded and maintained thanks to several securing points. (TB S-9720-15)

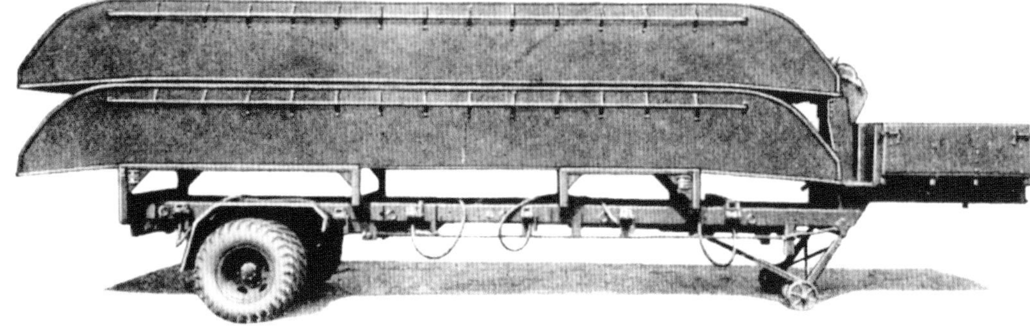

Below: As it had no big stowage chest, the entire length of the 25-ton Pontoon Trailer could be used to carry the bridge's apron. Built by four different manufacturers, there were some slight differences, more particularly with the mudguards. This example from the 89th Engineer Battalion is waiting for a truck tractor at the Fort Leonard Wood exercise zone, Missouri, January 13, 1942. (U.S. Army SC-133322/323)

have been identified. The standardization of the materiel meant that items with a low load capacity quickly became obsolete and the 25-ton version became more current.

25-Ton Pontoon Semitrailer

Built by the Fruehauf Trailer Company, the Dart Truck Company, the Electric Wheels Company, and the Trailer Company of America, this trailer was intended primarily for transporting parts of the floating bridge, classified as 25 ton, with various TMs identifying some 3,500 examples built. These trailers had a length of 299 inches (759.46 cm), a width of 98 inches (248.92 cm), and a height of 69½ inches (176.5 cm). They weighed 7,650 lb (3,476 kg) empty and could take a maximum weight of 18,000 lb (8,172 kg). The distribution of the full load had the tractor's fifth wheel take 8,978 lb (4,076 kg) and 16,675 lb (7,569 kg) on its only axle, with 12.00x20 14-ply twin tires—a distribution ratio of 35% to 65%.

Acetylene Gas Generator & Charging Plant Trailers

The high combustion heat level of acetylene meant very high temperatures could be reached (5792°F or 3200°C in pure oxygen) which makes it ideal for welding. A campaigning army must be able to make and store it in gas bottles. The trailer was made by Fruehauf and was fitted with equipment

Left and below: It was really only the technical specifications which differentiated these two semitrailers for 10- or 25-ton pontoons. (TB-9720-15)

Below left and right: There were a few small variations in the manufacturing of these semitrailers for producing acetylene; these were especially visible on the rear side of the trailer and the various ventilation grilles. (TM-5-5070)

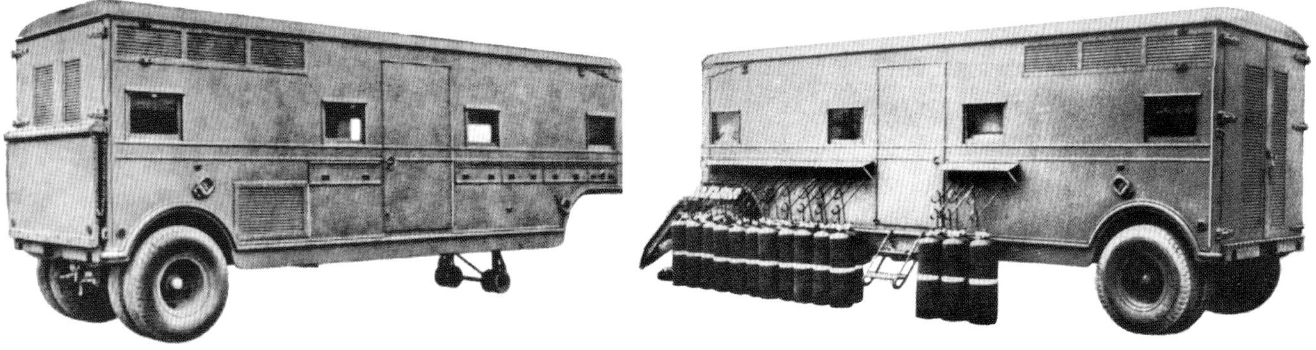

Left: Calcutta, India. This 94x43C Federal is towing an Oxygen-Nitrogen Gas Generator & Charging Plant Semitrailer from an LCT, in May 1944. (U.S. Army Air Forces ref. 63451-A.C.)

Above: Manila, Philippines, June 1, 1945. The 4th Repair Squadron of the USAAF at work. The men pose in front of the impressive apparatus used to fill the bottles with oxygen. (U.S. Army Air Forces ref. 63451-A.C.)

from Lindair Products, with a maximum yield of 750 cubic feet per hour (21 cubic meters).

These trailers with single axles and twin 12.00x20 14-ply wheels had a wheelbase of 290 inches (736.6 cm)—axle differential to the coupling point—for a total length of 354 inches (899.16 cm), a width of 99 inches (251.46 cm), and a height of 132 inches (335.28 cm).

Their maximum weight fully loaded was 31,859 lb (14,451 kg). The distribution of the mass had the fifth wheel of the tractor take 14,962 lb (6,787 kg) and 17,094 lb (7,754 kg) rested on the axle, a distribution ratio of 46% to 54%.

Below: The perfect illustration of coupling two trucks for towing heavy loads. Two U-8144-T Autocars have been linked together to provide the necessary power on the long, hilly portions of the Ledo Road, but also to increase the effectiveness of the braking and the speed modulations with the weight of the loads. (Private Collection)

Oxygen-Nitrogen Gas Generator & Charging Plant Trailers

As the welding processes needed a mixture of gases, the second of which was oxygen, these trailers complemented the preceding ones. Made by Heil, they were fitted with Independent Engineering equipment capable of yielding a maximum of 500 cubic feet per hour (14 cubic meters).

Apart from 12.00x20 16-ply twinned wheels, the basic features were the same as those of the Acetylene Gas Generator & Charging Plant Trailers.

Adventures in Burma: U-8144-T and the Locomotives

History is made of exploits big and small, some forgotten forever, others emerging from nothing. Four Pontoon Truck Tractors took part in a strange mission in deepest Asia, between India and Burma.

Among the American logistical units which are regularly ignored are the railway networks troops. Called the Railway Grand Divisions, they were made up of four to five Railway Battalions, each overseeing a line as well as ensuring the materiel and the infrastructures functioned well. To support each division was a Railway Shop Battalion. At the end of the war 11 Railway Grand Divisions were active in the various theaters of operations.

In January 1944, the 705th Railway Grand Division arrived in North East India, in the town of Guwahati, situated in Assam. Its 721st, 725th, 726th, 745th, and 748th Railway Battalions—plus the 758th Shop Battalion—operated a network of 810 miles (1,300 km) of railroads. In September 1944, the 758th Shop Battalion took delivery of two small diesel locomotives, which had to be taken to Burma by road, so they could participate in the

Left: The driver of the Autocar pulled too far to the left and the roadside yielded with the weight. Luckily, the second U-8144-T was able to stabilize the load before a bulldozer arrived. (Private Collection)

Below: Crossing watercourses was always with the help of a towing bulldozer. (Private Collection)

logistics flow at the end of the Ledo Road, toward China. No railway connection existed between the arrival and the departure points; moreover, at the time, the track gauges were different between regions in this part of Asia.

It was the Quartermaster Corps that was responsible for the land journey with the help of the Engineers. Made up mainly of four Pontoon Truck Tractors, two 20-ton Low Bed Semitrailers, two bulldozers and various support vehicles, the convoy set off for Mogaung in the north of Burma.

It was a journey of some 620 miles (1,000 km) undertaken along mountain trails and roads. It was done at a snail's pace, the speed based on that of the bulldozers and taking all the necessary precautions since the load of locomotives was high up and therefore the center of gravity was far from the ground. Almost two months were needed for this trip under exceptional conditions. When they reached their destination safe and sound, the two locomotives were unloaded on December 25, 1944.

Above: As soon as there was a serious accident on the vital artery that was the Ledo Road, all traffic stopped. Here GMCs, Autocars, Diamonds, Macks and Ward LaFrances wait patiently. By making a towing chain consisting of two U-8144-T and a bulldozer plus a lifting gantry on the back, the coupling was able to resume its route. (Private Collection)

Middle: The bulldozers also had the task of improving driving conditions by sorting out the tricky sections. (Private Collection)

Left: Mogaung, December 25, 1944. The locomotives reach their destination. All that is left to do is to put the locomotive wheels back on so they become operational again. (U.S. Army SC-193738)

U-8144-T Autocar

The United States Navy was not accustomed to using specialized vehicles created for the Army, but the U-8144-T Autocar was an exception.

In 1942, the U.S. Navy turned its attention to a vehicle in the 5/6-ton 4x4 Autocar range to look after its aircraft and get rid of the wrecks on the runways.

The U-8144-T Pontoon Truck Tractor became the U-8244-T Crash Crane Truck Tractor. The Navy Bureau of Aeronautics addressed its contract NXs-5056 to the Autocar firm to supply 90 vehicles, with 30 vehicles delivered in 1942 and 60 in 1943. Although the exterior appearance was the same as the U-8144-T, the U-8244-T was different.

With a wheelbase of 156 inches (396.24 cm), or 7½ inches (19.05 cm) shorter, it was a bit more compact. As it only had to move around on airfields, its fuel tank contained only 30 gallons (113.5 liters), giving it a range of 160 miles (256 km). With its crane, the truck now weighed 21,290 lb (9,665 kg), an increase in the mass of 4,695 lb (2,130 kg) compared with the pontoon truck. Note also the installation of direction indicators fitted just in front of the side flaps for ventilating the cabin.

Its crane was made by Gar Wood Industries; its boom was telescopic, ranging between 14 and 22 feet (4.27 m and 6.71 m). With its boom extended minimally and sloping at 60°, the U-8244-T had a maximum lift of 16,000 lb (7,264 kg). In its least favorable position, extended to 22 feet and inclined at 10°, the truck's lifting power was only 6,000 lb (2,724 kg).

Above: Velia Lavella Island, December 20, 1943, during an exercise with the remains of a decommissioned plane. Although the crane seems like the two installed on the 7½-ton 6x6 C-2s, it was however from another category. During the Pacific War, the island was the base for VMF-214, the squadron commanded by Gregory "Pappy" Boyington. (U.S. Navy)

Left: The island of Belio in Tarawa Atoll. On the side of the runway, the rapid intervention team is ready for any sort of accident. (U.S. Navy)

6

7½-Ton Truck Tractor Category

Ordered by the U.S. Army Air Forces, these special vehicles were not regulated by TMs, but by Technical Orders (TOs) like an aircraft or its components.

This particularity made the inventory of the models, the numbers ordered and/or effectively delivered very difficult to establish. Nine Technical Orders, all published in various versions, enable us to obtain a view of the two trucks produced: the C-2 Wrecking Truck Tractor Crane Truck and the Type F-1 Fuel Servicing Truck Tractor Tanker. It is certain that there was an overall minimum production of 5,789 7½-ton Tractor Trucks built jointly by three companies: the Biederman Motor Co., the Reo Motor Car Co., and the Federal Motor Truck Co.

A total of 2,677 Type C-2 Wrecking Tractor Trucks were identified with five quite clear series of registration numbers, the first three like traditional vehicles (USA-W-51489 to USA-W-51554, USA-W-54162 to USA-W-54477, and USA-W-58038 to USA-W-59896) with the next two as breakdown vehicles (USA-W-004272 to USA-W-004337 and USA-W-00107719 to USA-W-00108079), all these registration numbers being allocated to the Federal firm. The last series (USA-W-51005 to USA-W-51014) was allocated to Biederman trucks.

There were 3,112 Type F-1 Fuel Servicing Tractor Trucks identified with eight series of registration numbers, five for Biederman (USA-W-51435 to

Port Hueneme, California, a forest of booms. All these C-2 Wrecking Trucks photographed on May 24, 1946 have been assembled for an exceptional sale to civilians, with one condition: that the buyers be accredited veterans who want to create their own business or enlarge an existing company. (ACME ref. 25255)

Left: A detail specific to the Biederman trucks: the ventilation ducts on the side of the hood. (TO 19-25-54)

USA-W-51488, USA-W-52764 to USA-W-52928, USA-W-54678 to USA-W-54907, USA-W-59897 to USA-W-59999, and USA-W-51000 to USA-W-51400,), two series for Reo (USA-529278 to USA-531317, and USA-513000 to USA-5130218), and one series for Federal (USA-54478 to USA-54677).

Early F-1s and C-2s

These vehicles appeared in 1939, at the same time as the Air Forces were beginning to evolve.

When multi-engined aircraft entered service in huge numbers, they created fresh needs for breakdowns and resupply. The Corbitt Company received the first orders and was thus able to shape the image and form of the new F-1s and C-2s with pre-series vehicles. Four C-2 Wrecking Tractor Trucks with registration numbers between USA-W-5742 and USA-W-5745 were ordered, as were five F-1 Fuel Servicing Tractor Trucks, registered from USA-W-5737 and USA-W-5741.

As well as these nine first Corbitts, an accompanying order was sent to Biederman for two C-2s, given the registration numbers USA-W-5781 and USA-W-5782. The collaboration of Corbitt on this project for the Air Force 6x6s did not go much further, a last order for 12 F-1s, USA-W-5769 to USA-W-5780, was a sort of consolation prize.

Particularities

The trucks produced by the four builders involved in the 7½-ton 6x6 truck program all had their specific differences like the logo, the shape of the front wings and ventilation gills on the hood and other small details. But a manufacturing particularity differentiated the F-1 Tanker Trucks from the C-2 Wreckers. The width of the cabin of the former was less than that of the latter; in the simple tractor version it was barely wider (60 inches/152 cm) than the chassis whereas on the Wrecker, it stuck out almost to the edge of the running board (84 inches/213.36 cm). This was due to the crew—men sitting three abreast in the F-1 and four abreast in the C-2 of whom one sat to the left of the driver.

Below: The centerpiece of the forward structure of the bodywork, the radiator support with the protective grille either added or integrated, bears the builder's logo. Three letters embedded in the ensemble for Reo, a small rectangular insert for Federal or, as here, a triangle for Biederman. This inscription was often the only way of identifying the manufacturer. (TO 19-25-54)

Right: With Reo, the brand's three letters were borne proudly at the top of the radiator and, as with Federal, the sides of the hood were pierced by four large-grilled gills. These various particularities were visible as on the C-2. (Reo)

Top left: A first-generation Corbitt F-1 Fuel Servicing Tractor Truck; only five examples were bought under the designation of U.S. Army Air Corps 50SD6 Fuel Service. Their design originated directly from the civilian vehicles of the 1938/39 period. They were equipped with an HXC Hercules engine rated at 198 bhp.

Top right: The second order for Corbitt 50SD6s was for only 12 vehicles with cleaner lines, but with similar technical features, except for the power of the HXC engines which was reduced to 165 bhp. Their wheelbase was 180 inches (457.2 cm).

Above: Identical to the five first 50SD6s, this C-2 Wrecking Tractor Truck only existed in only four examples under the designation Corbitt 54SD6. These were the only examples made by this builder in this configuration with a crane and a lifting capacity of 15 tons.

Right: Biederman produced only two examples of the crane truck. It was fitted with an HXD Hercules rated at 184 bhp. Its crane only had a 10-ton capacity. (U.S. Army signal Corps)

F-1 Fuel Servicing Tractor Truck

There were 3,112 examples of this vehicle—all 7½-ton 6x6 trucks—reserved for the Air Force only and they were built by three companies.

Above: Hickam Field on Oahu Island, Hawaii in 1949, this F-1 Fuel Servicing Tractor Truck and its F-1A Fuel Servicing Tractor Truck refuel a Douglas C-54. The vehicle and its trailer bear the insignia of the Air Transport Command (U.S. Army Air Forces A-40871)

The initial design of this model was made in 1939 with a few rare examples built by the Corbitt Company with the reference Model 50SD6. Series production was finally entrusted to the Biederman Motors Co., the Reo Motor Car Co., and the Federal Motor Truck. The job of the F-1 Servicing Tractor Trucks was to supply the fleets of big aircraft. The tractor was thus associated with the F-1 or F-1A 4,000-gallon (15,000-liter) Fuel Servicing Semitrailer.

These F1 Fuel Servicing Trucks are a good example of the nomenclatures of the Army and their applications. Classified as 7½ US long tons or the equivalent of 16,800 lb (7,627 kg) payload, they could take twice that weight. Apart from its offroad use, when the truck was on the road, the payload and the towing capacity were doubled in theory and the F1s were considered as 15-long-ton trucks. This was not applicable to the vehicles that could not change into six-wheel drive like these 6x6 trucks.

Left: September 1944 on French roads. To supply its ground forces, the Air Force took part in the Red Ball Express with the ensembles made up of an F-1 Truck and two F-1A Semitrailers. (U.S. Army SC-332041)

On the road or simply on the huge airstrips, it was not unusual to see the F-1s towing two semitrailers, the second of which rested on a dolly.

The Shape

The F-1s were quite traditional semitrailer tractors with the cabin behind the engine compartment and a technical part on the fifth wheel. Based on a chassis with two main longerons and six crossmembers, this outfit had three differentials with a wheelbase of 196 inches (497.84 cm). Built only with a hardtop cabin, the tractor was 104 inches (264.16 cm) high, 94.5 inches (240.03 cm) wide, and 283 inches (718.82 cm) long.

Weighing 27,500 lb (12,485 kg) net, the F-1 could tow semitrailers with a maximum weight of 65,000 lb (29,510 kg) but not carry more than 16,000 lb (7,264 kg) on the tractor's fifth wheel. The braking system, working also for the trailers or the haulage, was of the Westinghouse Automotive Air Brake System compressed-air type. It was fed by a compressor located on the left-hand side of the engine block, the air produced being stocked in the two cylindrical tanks within the chassis. Quick-fitting couplings for the trailer brakes were located directly behind the cabin.

Above: This example of an F-1 which proudly bears the Reo brand on its front, refuels a B-29. The bright yellow finish was specified for vehicles operating on the runways. (U.S. Army Air Forces)

Left: Iwo Jima and its impressive air base. The B-29's proportions made it easier to use four fuel tankers to fill up. (U.S. Army Air Forces 59046 A.C.)

Below: An F-1 refueling a B-24 on the island of Angaur, October 6, 1944. (U.S. Army Air Forces 64136 A.C.)

The Mechanics

Using 10.00x23, 12-ply tires, the F-1 rested on a Timken-Detroit F-3200-W front differential and two tandem type Timken-Detroit SD-3000-PA ensembles with 75350-PA- and 75351-PA-type differentials.

The vehicle was powered by an XHD Hercules gasoline engine in a single block housing six pistons. It had a capacity of 855 cubic inches (14,014 cc), rated at 180 bhp at 2,600 rpm. It was water cooled by a radiator made up of vaned tubes and a water pump located on the front of the engine block, ventilation being by means of a six-bladed fan to increase the cooling of its 60 quarts (56.76 liters) which constituted the cooling circuit. Note that the first Reos and Biedermans were powered by the HXC block rated at only 160 bhp.

Transferring the engine drive through a clutch was by means of a 7851 Spicer gearbox with five forward and one reverse gears, and a T-77-3 Wisconsin two-stage transfer box. With these mechanics and a 60-gallon (227.10-liter) fuel tank, in two fuel tanks installed on each side of the chassis, it had a range of between 180 miles (290 km) in its solo configuration and 150 miles (240 km) coupled

Above: The maximum configuration for this F-1 Fuel Servicing Truck and its two Fuel Servicing F-1A Semitrailers. The ensemble is 75 feet 6 inches (23 m) long for a total payload of 52 tons. (U.S. Army Air Forces)

Middle: A near-miss avoided just in time when fire broke out in this Fuel Servicing Semitrailer's pumping machinery. As soon as everything was extinguished and had cooled down, the contents were transferred to another tanker semitrailer towed by a Biederman F-1. (Private Collection).

Right: A Federal F-1 from the end of production with the protective radiator grill inserted into the ensemble of the radiator grille. (U.S. Army Air Forces 23920 A.C.)

with a maximum payload, a consumption rate of between 2.50 and 3 mpg, this consumption varying with the type of road, the running conditions, and the configuration—whether towing or not.

All the electrics worked on a 6-volt system with a positive earth, from two 6-volt batteries arranged in parallel, except for starting the engine which worked with a 12-volt starter. It was thanks to the electrical circuit of the ignition contactor, which alone was fed by the two batteries in series via an electromagnetic contactor, that this differentiation was possible. Most of the electrical parts were made by Auto-Lite.

A lot of particularities completed the F-1 ensemble, like powered steering via a cylinder linked to the compressed air, front suspension equipped with two pneumatic cylinders, and a manual inertia starter.

Evolution

The F-1 evolved in different ways. The first examples came directly from civilian trucks with the militarization being on the radiator grille.

There were covers for the headlights installed on the side, and the installation of small marker lights with bluish lenses on the top of the wings. The second version was given a new hood with a protective grille incorporated into the supporting structure of the radiator and a rounder design, meaning that the hood had to be reprofiled. The headlights rested on the wings with an individual grille, and the modification of the electrical cabling was put to profit to suppress the three small central lights on the top of the cabin. Meanwhile, the blackout drive and the blackout fender lights completed the vehicle's militarization at the end of production; the dashboard received a few accessories like the fitting of a primary injection pump and various improvements for the accessory controls.

4,000-Gallon Fuel Servicing Semitrailers

Ordered so they could be coupled to the tractors that we have just described, these semitrailers with a 4,000-gallon (1,514-liter) capacity were very popular auxiliaries for the fleets of four-engined aircraft. There were two versions, the F-1 Fuel Servicing Trailer and the F-1A, the former having an aluminum tank and the latter a steel tank. Although they didn't look the same, they both had two individually motorized pumps with a flow rate of 320 gallons (1,211 liters) per minute. The braking system was by compressed air.

F-1 4,000-Gallon Fuel Servicing Semitrailer

These were trailers with a double axle and twin 10.00x22, 12-ply tires and a wheelbase of 185¾ inches (471.8 cm)—along the axis from the axle differential to the coupling point—for a total length of 360 inches (914.4 cm), a width of 96 inches (243.84 cm), and a height of 116 inches (296.22 cm). They weighed 16,455 lb (7,464 kg) empty and could take a maximum weight of 24,021 lb (10,896 kg).

Without any covering bodywork, the F-1 Semitrailer was easier to use and maintain. The Mariannas, July 1944. (U.S. Army Air Forces 63813 A.C.)

Left: The F-1, 4,000-gallon Fuel Servicing Semitrailer was an early model, and the F-1A was preferred to it. (TM 0-2800)

The distribution of the mass had the tractor's fifth wheel take 14,654 lb (6,647 kg) and 28,822 lb (11,713 kg) on its axle train, a distribution ratio of 36% to 64%.

F-1A 4,000-Gallon Fuel Servicing Semitrailer

These were trailers with a double axle and twin 10.00x22, 12-ply tires with a wheelbase of 185¾ inches (471.8 cm)—along the axis from the axle differential to the coupling point—for a total length of 360 inches (914.4 cm), a width of 96 inches (243.84 cm), and a height of 109 inches (276.22 cm). Weighing 19,693 lb (8,933 kg) empty, they could take a maximum weight of 24,021 lb (10,896 kg). The distribution of the mass had the tractor's fifth wheel take 17,211 lb (7,087 kg) and 28,822 lb (11,713 kg) on its axle train, a distribution ratio of 38% to 62%.

Below: At the front, we can see here the registration beginning with an O as in the case of trailers, Okinawa, June 7, 1945. (U.S. Army Air Forces 70393 A.C.)

Right: Just out of the factory, this C-2 Wrecking Truck Tractor proudly bears the three letters REO cast in the mass of the radiator grille. On this sole pre-series model, the headlights were high up and the protective grille of the radiator had two lateral protective "ears" in front of the road lights. (Private Collection)

C-2 Wrecking Tractor Truck

There were 2,677 examples of these Air Force crane trucks in the 6x6 7½-ton category produced by two builders.

As we have seen, the first examples were produced in a limited series in 1939 by Corbitt with the reference 54SD6. Series supply was assured by Biederman Motors Co. and Federal Motors Truck Co. A single pre-series vehicle was ordered from Reo.

Contrary to what the truck's overall shape would have us believe, it was not a breakdown truck which could be assimilated to the Army Wreckers. Except for the tower crane, the C-2 did not have any material and breakdown tooling, simply considered as semitrailer tractors with an extra means of handling, which enabled them to load and unload their trailer.

The C-2's job was clear: recovering crashed aircraft and towing trailers. The C-2 was very useful during maintenance and repair operations; its jib crane was an excellent means of handling, especially when an engine or a whole wing had to be replaced, or simply lifting a whole or part of an aircraft to enable work to be carried out.

During breakdowns involving removal and transport, the truck was uncoupled from its trailer so it was still mobile; it carried out all the crane operations which the loading needed and then the tractor-trailer duo was re-formed to transfer the load to the workshop or simply to remove the debris.

Below: The typical C-2 configuration with its 25-foot 12½-ton Wrecking Semitrailer. (Private Collection)

The Shape

These C-2s were traditional semitrailer tractors with the cabin behind the engine compartment and the technical part with a tower and fifth wheel at the rear. Based on a chassis with two main longerons and

Left: Designed before the arrival of the big four-engined aircraft, the C-2 with a short and curved jib was also large enough to carry out work on fighters or smaller twin-engined aircraft. But they rendered great service when handling heavy bombers. (U.S. Army Air Forces 50260 A.C.)

Below: To enable the operators to access the crane's controls, a retractable work platform was deployed. England 1944, on the 9151st Bomb Group, Eighth Air Force's airfield. (U.S. Army Air Forces A-49708)

six crossmembers, this outfit had three differentials with a wheelbase of 189½ inches (481.33 cm). Built only with a hardtop cabin, the tractor was 125 inches high (319.41 cm). It was 96½ inches (245.11 cm) wide and 405½ inches (1,029.97 cm) long, counting the tip of the jib. Weighing in all 28,000 lb (12,712 kg), the C-2 could tow semitrailers with a maximum weight of 39,000 lb (17,706 kg) but not carry more than 13,000 lb (5,902 kg) on the tractor's fifth wheel. The braking system, working also for the trailers or the haulage, was of the Westinghouse Automotive Air Brake System compressed-air type. It was fed by a compressor

Below: July 1943, North Africa. Repairing a Lockheed P-38, hit during a mission over Sicily. The C-2, still with a curved jib, has a new cast-iron grille incorporated into the bodywork. (U.S. Army Air Forces A-28992)

Right: To change a C-2 into a breakdown truck, the only space available for fitting the chests fixed to a structure was the cabin roof. Access to these tools was made easier by a metal ladder. Replacing the extinguishers on the running boards by bottles, the vehicle also had the means to cut and weld. This is a file-past for the war loans, probably at Lakewood in Washington State. (Private Collection)

located on the left-hand side of the engine block; the air produced was stocked in the two cylindrical tanks within the chassis. Quick-fitting couplings for the trailer brakes were located directly behind the crane tower, near the fifth wheel.

To carry out horizontal towing, a winch with a 7½-ton (6,810-kg) capacity was fitted to the truck rear, inside the chassis. For lifting operations, all the first examples were equipped with a Gar Wood tower crane with a lifting arm curved at its extremity and 15 feet (547.5 cm) long, the ensemble had a 10-ton (9,070-kg) capacity. The crane was controlled from a collapsible platform located at the rear left-hand side of the cabin, where the operator had three control levers at his disposal, one for moving the hook, one for pivoting the base of the jib, and one for regulating the inclination of the jib.

The Mechanics

Using 11.00x20 12-ply tires, the C-2 rested on an F-3200-W Timken-Detroit front differential and on two ensembles, also Timken-Detroits, SD-3000-PA tandem types, with 75350-PA and 75351-PA differentials. The vehicle was powered by an XHD Hercules gasoline engine in a single block housing six pistons. This ensemble had a capacity of 855 cubic inches (14,014 cc), rated at 180 bhp at 2,000 rpm. It was water cooled by a radiator made up of vaned tubes and a water pump located on the front of the engine block; ventilation was by means of a six-bladed fan to increase the cooling of its 60 quarts (56.76 liters) which made up the cooling circuit.

Note that the first Reo and Biederman examples were powered by the HXC block rated at only 160 bhp. Transferring the engine drive through a clutch was by means of a 7851 Spicer gearbox with five forward and one reverse gears, and a T-77-3 Wisconsin two-stage transfer box. With these

Below: January 23, 1944, New Guinea. Artisanal but effective, this gantry attached to the crane and fastened to the towing hook of the truck enabled a plane to be lifted and its wheels replaced. (U.S. Army Air Forces A-49708)

mechanics, a 110-gallon (416.35-liter) reserve in two tanks located on each side of the chassis behind the cabin access running boards, gave the C-2 a range of between 330 miles (530 km) in its solo configuration and 150 miles (240 km) all coupled up with full payload, or a consumption rate of between 1½ and 3 mpg, this consumption varying with the type of road, the running conditions, and the configuration—whether towing or not.

All the truck's electrics worked on 6 volts with a positive earth from two 6-volt batteries arranged in parallel, except for starting the engine which worked with a 12-volt starter. It was thanks to the electrical circuit of the ignition contactor, which alone was fed by the two batteries in series via an electromagnetic contactor, that this differentiation was possible. Most of the electrical parts were made by Auto-Lite.

The C-2 ensemble also benefitted from power assisted steering via a cylinder linked to compressed air and a front suspension equipped with two big pneumatic cylinders. Two big work headlights

Above: The capacity of the C-2 was not strong enough to lift a B-17 entirely. As soon as the ground crews of the 92 Bomb Group have pumped out the fuel tanks, it will be possible to remove the wing and engines. England, May 2, 1945. (U.S. Army Air Forces 75986 A.C.)

Right and below: To address this B-24 bogged down on the side of the runway, two C-2s are needed. Step by step, the cranes are able to reposition it on its undercarriage and tow it. American Air Base at Poltava, USSR, January 12, 1945. (U.S. Army Air Forces 70132 A.C.)

were powered with 110 volts from a small 3 kW electric generator located on the inside of the crane structure. It was able to supply electricity for any tooling or lighting used during a breakdown. On the radiator front, there was a manual inertia starter.

Evolution

The radiator grille, the headlights, the various lights, the shape of the hood, as well as the dashboard all evolved like the F-1.

With the introduction of bigger and bigger machines, the crane truck could no longer lift a plane or handle even heavier elements, which required greater lifting capacity of the jib. The C-2 was modified, the power of the crane was reduced to 5 tons (4,535 kg) and the jib became straightened and telescopic in three positions: 18, 22, and 26 feet (549 cm, 671 cm, and 793 cm).

Wrecking Semitrailers

Designed for the C-2 Tractor, these semitrailers with long decks were intended for transporting damaged aircraft or their main elements. They had different lengths, but their payloads were similar.

25-Foot Model Wrecking Semitrailer

These were semitrailers with a double axle and 10.00x15, 12-ply tires, and a wheelbase of 344 inches (873.76 cm)—axis of the tandem axle to the coupling point—for a total length of 420 inches (1,066.8 cm), a width of 97 inches (246.38 cm), and a height of 93 inches (236.22 cm). Weighing 11,009 lb (4,994kg) empty, they could take a maximum weight of 25,029 lb (11,353 kg). The distribution of the mass had the tractor's fifth wheel take 12,010 lb (5,448 kg) and 24,028 lb (10,899 kg) on its axle, a distribution ratio of 33% to 67%.

Top: The right inclination of the jib associated to the faultless distribution of the truck's mass offered an ensemble that could lift a P-51 and retract the undercarriage leg which had survived the crash. (U.S. Army Air Forces 122075 A.C.)

Middle: A C-2 handling new engines in a Service Group at Ondal Army Air Base, India 1943. (U.S. Army Air Forces 67302 A.C.)

Bottom: March 15, 1945, 382nd Base Unit, India. Periodic maintenance for a Curtiss C-46's engines. (U.S. Army Air Forces 73313 A.C.)

Left: Nouméa, New Caledonia at the 13th Air Depot. All hitched up to 4/5-ton 4x4 Truck Tractors, various trailers are parked in the foreground. From left: two 15-ton Carryall Semitrailers, two 29-foot Wrecking Semitrailers, and three 40-foot Wrecking Semitrailers. (U.S. Army Air Forces 71584 A.C.)

40-Foot Model Wrecking Semitrailer

The axles and the wheels were identical but the wheelbase was 488 inches (1,239.52 cm)—axis of the tandem axle to the coupling point—for a total length of 600 inches (1,524 cm), a width of 96 inches (243.84 cm), and a height of 109 inches (276.86 cm). Weighing 13,011 lb (5,902 kg) empty, they could take a maximum weight of 24,021 lb (10,896 kg). The distribution of the mass had the tractor's fifth wheel take 13,011 lb (5,902 kg) and 24,224 lb (10,988 kg) on its axle, a distribution ratio of 35% to 65%.

Below: Direction Stateside for this V-2 resting on a 40-foot trailer. Prepared for a long trip to port, the C-2 Wrecking Semitrailer has been provided a lot of jerrycans. (U.S. Army Air Forces 71584 A.C.)

Bottom: Loaded with a North American T-6, this 40-foot Wrecking Semitrailer is largely over-dimensioned for this type of machine. (Private Collection)

12-Ton Truck Tractor Category

A vehicle for a single purpose, the 12-ton 6x6 Truck Tractor had only one job: recovering light and medium damaged or broken-down tanks.

In mid-1941, the Ordnance Department defined the broad outlines of its project. It opted for a 6x6 truck towing a semitrailer. The vehicle had to be able to carry out all the loading and recovery operations even if the armored vehicle was unable to move, provided the terrain and any road permitted it. A speed of 35 mph (56 kph) with a full payload had to be possible. Moreover, the vehicle's cabin had to be able to house all the crew and be armored to provide a minimum of protection on the battlefield.

It was the Dart Motor Truck Co. that presented the first examples of a vehicle with the traditional silhouette, the T-13 Heavy Wrecker, one with an open cabin and the other with an armored cabin. Associated with the new T-28 semitrailer, the T-3 Tank Recovery Unit was formed.

The design with the cabin behind the powerplant gave it a very long hood and a 201-inch (510.86-cm) wheelbase needing a much-reinforced chassis which underwent various changes, thought excessive. The distribution of the mass—far from being ideal—was too restrictive and wore the mechanics down prematurely and made the vehicle difficult to maneuver.

At the same time, the Knuckey Truck Co. proposed a slightly different design, a COE, enabling the wheelbase to be reduced by 29 inches (73.98 cm) to 172 inches (436.88 cm). This was a more comfortable driving solution, given there was no hood. Designated as Truck Tractor T-25 in June 1942, the prototype was delivered in September. If globally the T-25 had the general outline of the Dart model, the comparison stopped there. The T-25's real innovation was in the power transmission to the rear drive wheels. Finished the fragile wheel shafts, they were replaced by a system of gears and a chain lubricated drop by drop on the outside of the chassis. The truck was also fitted with a complex compressed-air braking system. Activated by the brake pedal, it acted on the rear tandem wheels, but the driver also activated three levers installed on the steering wheel column, which allowed for using the brakes independently, by acting either on the left-hand wheels or the right-hand wheels, or simply on those of the trailer.

Despite the overweight problem on the front differential which had not been solved, the T-25 Truck Tractor had elements with increased power compared with the T-13. The front winch had a capacity of 35,000 lb (15,890 kg) and the double winch in tandem at the rear of the cabin 2 x 60,000 lb (2 x 27,240 kg). But it was not the vehicle's technical

The T-25 Truck Tractor by the Knuckey Truck Company gave rise to the range of the M26s made by the Pacific Car and Foundry Co. Presented here without the last accessory, it almost had its definitive form. (U.S. Army ORD-16881)

Above and left: Be they with an open cabin or an armored cabin, the Heavy Wreckers from the Dart Motor Truck Co, were called the T-13s. The first tractor was given the registration number USA-W-007988 and the second USA-W-007988, the double zero prefix designating them as breakdown trucks. (U.S. Army ORD-62893/72672)

features that posed a problem for the Knuckey Truck Co. Indeed, its small size meant it was not awarded the contract. It had to be content with supplying elements of the rear tandem wheels to the company designated by the Army.

Pacific M26s

The Army quickly chose between the T-13 and the T-25: it preferred the latter, but found that the production capacity of the Knuckey Truck Co. was inadequate and ordered the new vehicle from the Pacific Car amd Foundry Co.

This company worked on the vehicle, completing its cabin, and used ¾-inch (1.9-cm) armor steel for the front part, while the sides, the rear and the roof were made of ¼-inch (0.64-cm) steel. It made the electrical installation conform to Army standards, adding to it the welding and cutting equipment, fitting it with a base for the spare wheel's removable bracket, and installing several attachment points. It fitted several accessories like the exhaust pipe protection, towbars, and pioneer's tools. The M26 Truck Tractor was made in 1943 and 1944 with respectively 300 and 453 examples. Administratively considered as armor, this truck did not have a traditional chassis number attributed by its manufacturer. Like all tanks and halftracks, it was the Ordnance Department that gave it a serial number, stamped on its chassis.

The Shape

These Pacific M26s were semitrailer tractors of the COE type with a technical part on a fifth wheel; its dimensions enabled it to protect the seven crewmembers. Based on a chassis with two main longerons and five crossmembers, this outfit with its three differentials had a wheelbase of 172 inches (436.88 cm). Built only with an armored cabin, the

tractor was 118 inches high (299.72 cm), 13½ inches (331.47 cm) wide, and 307 inches (779.78 cm) long. Weighing in all 48 895 lb (22,198 kg), the M426 could tow semitrailers with a maximum weight on the road of 117,500 lb (53,345 kg) but not carry more than 60,000 lb (27,240 kg) on the tractor's fifth wheel. The braking system, working also for the trailers or the haulage, was of the Westinghouse Automotive Air Brake System compressed-air type

The Mechanics

Using 14.00x16-, 20-, or 24-ply tires, the M26 rested on a F-7900-A752 Timken-Detroit front differential, and on two ensembles of the tandem type with 1828-82 Timken-Detroit differentials. The vehicle was powered by a 440 Hall-Scott turbocharged gasoline engine in a single block housing six pistons. It had a capacity of 1,090 cubic

Top: In jubilant Le Mans, September 18, 1944, an M26 tows an M4 Medium Tank on its trailer. The crew of this early-production example has replaced the original headlights with blackout equipment. (U.S. Army SC-194387)

Above: Several accessories allowed for various types of breakdown. The towing triangle allowed a tank simply to be towed. Bastogne perimeter, December 30, 1944, with elements of the 4th Armored Division. (U.S. Army SC-197936)

Left: The use of the incorporated hoisting rig on uneven terrain enabled a tank to be lifted and this made recovery easier. England, January 24, 1944 during an exercise carried out with pyrotechnics. (U.S. Army SC-280109)

September 1944 at the Ordnance Operation–Engineering Standards Vehicle Laboratory in Detroit. This M26 from mid-production bears the serial numbers 383 and the registration number USA-547826, which associated it with a series of 295 vehicles ordered under the contract number W-883-ORD-2479 where it was in second place. (U.S. Army Ordnance)

Above left: If all the openings of the cabin had an armored shutter, only the front side was fitted with two removable glassed-in parts. This example was incorporated into the 128th Armored Maintenance Ordnance Battalion of the 6th Armored Division. (Private Collection)

Above right: December 4, 1944, in the 84th Infantry Division zone, a Pacific of the 464th Ordnance Company easily tows the 44 tons of a trackless Panther. The handling jib has been mounted on the spare wheel. (U.S. Army SC-280109)

inches (17,885 cc), rated at 270 bhp at 2,100 rpm. It was water cooled by a radiator made up of vaned tubes and a water pump located on the front of the engine block, ventilation being by means of a six-bladed fan to increase the cooling of its 56 quarts (52.98 liters) which constituted the cooling circuit. Transferring the engine drive through a clutch was by means of a gearbox with four forward and one reverse gears, and a secondary box with three gears and a transfer box. With these mechanics and with a 100-gallon (378.5-liter) fuel tank in two fuel tanks fitted on either side of chassis, it had a range of 100 miles (160 km) towing and with a full payload and a consumption rate of 1 mpg, this consumption varying with the type of road, the running conditions, and the configuration—whether towing or not.

Pacific M26A1

The M26 Truck Tractor evolved but in the present case, this change was not due to normal technical developments but from a change in direction, aiming to perpetuate a concept.

A lot of reasons could be put forward to justify the M26 being transformed. At first, the way operations were going meant that armored-cabin trucks no longer needed to be built. As a result, economies were being made on strategic materials while reducing the abnormally large limits on the mechanics of the front train, among which was early tire wear caused by the excess weight of the armored cabin.

In May 1944, tests were carried out with an M26 without its armor and in October, the unarmored version was standardized with the designation M26A1 Truck Tractor, reclassifying the M26 as Limited Standard (meaning it was supplied until stocks ran out, and no longer produced).

The basic vehicle remained the same; only the front bodywork was entirely redesigned. Replacing the armor plating with rigid bodywork increased the internal volume; the lateral mudguards disappeared in favor of complete wheel arches. The weight saved was considerable between the two versions; the truck went on a diet and lost almost one and a half tons, the result also of the roof being made of canvas on a tubular structure, which also supported the circular ring mount of the .50-caliber machine gun.

A multitude of details also differentiate between the two vehicles; tool chests were placed on the side, on the front of the vehicle to receive the pioneers' lots; soft sides with integrated windows now protected the cabin openings, and the searchlight was installed on the top of the front face.

The context of the M26A1's use seemed also to be different; note that the blackout lighting disappeared, and the vehicles were assigned in a more centralized way to the Ordnance Evacuation Companies.

These elements would encourage us to suppose that the M26A1 was no longer a vehicle intended for use near the front lines, but more for the rear zones, where it did not need either special lighting or armor when used. There were 619 M26A1s ordered, 275 in 1944, and 344 in 1945. During the next decade they were fitted with a 24-volt system replacing the 12-volt one, which gave it a new designation M26A2 Truck Tractor.

Production

Although the rigor, quite military, of the American documents can be considered as an example, it happened that the way operations evolved forced the Ordnance Department to sort out its orders and its registers. The M26 and M26A1s were a good example of this confusion. It seems that orders had been prepared for 2,765 vehicles: 2,294 M26s and 471 M26A1s. The production reports covering the period of May 1943 to August 1945 only mention 1,372 examples, without distinguishing between the two models, but the Acceptances indicate the following allocation, 753 M26s and 619 M26A1s, without being able to compare them with the series of registration numbers assigned to these trucks.

This imbroglio can only be unraveled by comparing the numbers on the orders with those on the production reports, and establishing the table following, without considering the purchases of new M26A1s after August 1945, or with registrations which had not been used for other vehicles or new numbers attributed postwar.

Top: Despite being totally redesigned, the M26A1 still gave the impression of strength and power. (Private Collection)

Middle and bottom: *Miss America* was an early-production M26A1 as shown by its registration number made up of seven figures. Its dedicated trailer was the M15A1. (Private Collection)

Right: February 1945 in the port of Antwerp, loading a new T-26E3 Pershing tank onto an M26A1 Truck Tractor and a reinforced M15 Semitrailer. The whole ensemble kept the appellation Tank Recovery Unit M25. (U.S. Army SC-200736)

Right: Camp Campbell, Kentucky in 1948. Transporting an M39 Utility Car, this ensemble is made up of the M15A1 of the semitrailer. (U.S. Army SC-315128)

Below: Although it is not the cabin which is new, by becoming the M26A1, the Pacific kept all the mechanical elements and all its breakdown capacities. This bird's-eye view can be compared with the shot on page 127.

Above left: Quite visible, the structure is made up of a mix of tubes with the double job of supporting the canvas protection against bad weather and the circular gun mount for the antiaircraft machine gun.

Above right: With the absence of blackout lighting, the M26A1's headlights were fitted with metal shutters. As with the roofing, the sides of the cabin were protected by flexible windows. (U.S. Army Signal Corps)

Production of M26 & M26A1 Truck Tractors by the Pacific Car & Foundry Co., 1943–45

Quantity	Orders	registration Numbers	Comments
300	W-883-ORD-2479	536500 to 536799	Serial numbers 1 to 300, all M26 delivered in 1943
80		545562 to 545641	Serial numbers 302 to 381, all M26 delivered in 1944
295		547825 to 548119	Serial numbers 382 to 676, all M26 delivered in 1944
407	ORD-04-200-96	597971 to 598377	78 examples M26 delivered in 1944
			275 examples M26A1 delivered in 1944
			54 examples M26A1 delivered in 1945
79	W-883-ORD-2479	5122321 to 5122399	290 examples M26A1 delivered in 1945
133		5123321 to 5123453	
1,000		5136071 to 5137070	
80	Unknown	5147301 to 5147380	None delivered
391		5147381 to 5147771	
Of a total of 2,765 12-ton 6x6 Truck Tractors ordered, only 1,372 were delivered (753 M26s and 619 M26A1s) with 1,393 undelivered.			

M15 & M15A1 Semitrailers

Although the M26 and M26A1 Truck Tractors were adequate for their jobs and could adapt to the evolution of the new armored vehicles, the same could not be said of their indispensable trailers.

During its existence, the trailer underwent transformations to keep it up to the same level and perform better and better.

T-28/M15 Semitrailer

Created at the same time as the truck, even if it was by two different companies, the T-28 Semitrailer built by Fruehauf Trailer Co., depended on the wheels that were fitted to it. Because of their large diameter, it was necessary, while maintaining the lowest profile for the trailer—for among other things the center of gravity—to have the tank tracks pass between the double tires. The T-28 was therefore calibrated to the axial gauge of the M3/M5 Light Tank tracks which was 73½ inches (186.69 cm) and of the M3/M4 Medium Tank which was 83 inches (210.82 cm). Only these two categories of armor were in use at the time of the study and the orders. Still with the spirit of balance, the width of the trailer's running surface was pushed to its technical possible maximum in this configuration with 150 inches (381 cm). In these circumstances, the lateral dimensions could

Above: Desert Training Center in California, January 29, 1943. Though not yet in production, the Truck Tractor and the Semitrailer finish their evaluation. (U.S. Army SC-165202)

Right: First big evolution for the M15: the raceways have been reinforced, and big blocks of wood have been placed between the wheels. (ORD-A3516)

Below: Lateral closeup on an early-production M15 Semitrailer. It had no protection for its tires, which meant that tank tracks had to pass through the pairs of twin wheels. (U.S. Army Signal Corps)

The tracks of this LVT-2 moving across the tires of this M15 were quick to wear down the rubber of this first-generation vehicle. The Netherlands, March 10, 1945. (U.S. Army SC-202365)

be reduced to 124 inches (341.96 cm), this operation being carried out by tightening augers acting on the positioning of the balance wheels. This particularity was practical for going over or under narrow bridges or for using the Engineers' crossing methods whose width was not more than 133 inches (340 cm) at the time. The TM 9-2800-1 also noted that this particularity was essential for sea transport, to save as much space as possible.

The T-28 Semitrailer was a trailer of the hammock-type with the load being placed between the swan's neck and the rear running gear, with 53% of the loads borne by the axles and 47% resting on the tractor. These two parts were linked by two self-supporting running tracks, the space between these zones being used for stowage chests protected laterally by longitudinal platform drop skids. When it was not hitched up, the trailer rested on two support legs which could be folded up under it for the running configuration.

Production of M15 Semitrailers by Fruehauf Trailer Co.			
Quantity	Orders	registration Numbers	Comments
300	W-374-ORD-1672	0128362 to 0128661	Serial numbers 3 to 302, all delivered in 1943
80		0494100 to 0494179	Serial numbers 303 to 382, 76 delivered in 1943 and 4 in 1944
295		0546949 to 0547243	Serial numbers 383 to 677, all delivered in 1944
407		0741047 to 0741453	Serial numbers 678 to 1084, 350 delivered in 1944 and 57 in 1945
79		0817703 to 0817781	Serial numbers 1085 to 1163, all delivered in 1945
133	ORD-20-18-7023	0920351 to 0920483	Serial numbers 1166 to 1298, all delivered in 1945
Or a total of 1,294 M15 Semitrailers.			

What differentiated this semitrailer from all those used by the Army was the great quantity of accessories needed for recovering tanks: a lot of anchor points, various drums for the winch guiding cables installed on the truck, two removable ramps, and all the tooling required for handling and securing the loads located in the chests installed in the thickness of the raceways.

The M15A1 was given two sets of half-ramps for protecting its tires; it was also reinforced on the sides which dispensed with its stowage chests. (U.S. Army Signal Corps)

Above: The appearance of the M15A1 tank solved all the loading difficulties, especially when the tank had broken down and it could not itself pass over the obstacle of the trailer wheels. (U.S. Army SC-379421)

The M15 also had specific items for recovering armor which were used to guide the tank while it was being winched onto the trailer. Four protective wheel skid guards for the inner tires were placed on top of the swan's neck, and two removable skids hooked onto the loading ramps were positioned on the central tray. It was here that the elements of the crane were to placed; this was a jib and a rail on which the manual winch slid. Used for handling heavy elements (and the spare wheel), it could be positioned in four different places on the trailer, two at the front and two near the rear wheels.

But when the heavier and more voluminous tanks arrived, the M15 rapidly reached its limit. The new vehicles could no longer climb onto the trailer without crushing the tires and weighed close to the maximum payload.

In April 1944, the Ordnance Department recommended part of the M15 being modified. The swan's neck was reinforced by placing heavy steel plates on the lateral stairs, the archways near the tire trains were given impressive, beveled blocks so that the tracks would pass over the wheels, and the running tracks were also reinforced with thick plates. These modifications meant no changes in the military designation. M15 production was spread out over 1943, 1944, and 1945 with respective productions of 376, 649, and 269 examples, and with a load-bearing capacity of 80,000 lb (36,320 kg).

M15A1 Semitrailer

The arrival of the new M4A3-E2 Sherman tanks with their reinforced armor, of the T26E3 Pershings and other heavy machines at the end of the war meant that the M15 had to evolve, improved models being no longer sufficient. The loading bed was reinforced with side beams, thus suppressing the tool chests, and four removable half-ramps positioned to protect the rear tires. 916 examples of this semitrailer were ordered in two series of registration numbers, USA-0920484 to USA-0921183 and USA-01112238 to USA-1112454, but only 110 units were delivered in 1945, the others were delivered afterward. They were all homologated for an authorized payload of 90,000 lb (40,860 kg). Their serial numbers were from 1299 and 2214.

Below: England, March 1944. Maneuvers preparing for operations in Normandy pushed materiel to limit and toughened up the crews. (U.S. Army Signal Corps)

8

20-Ton Truck Tractor Category

Federal 604

Delivered between 1942 and 1944, these heavy road tractors for transporting light armor were produced by two firms.

The creation of these trucks was in parallel with those of the Diamond T M20 and answered the British Army's large demand. Apart from the towing method and the trailer's configuration, they were both intended to transport armored vehicles over long distances. They had one point in common: a 4MB Mead Morrison Gar Wood winch.

The winch's capability was 25,000 lb (11,350 kg) and was installed on the chassis, just behind the cabin. Its main use was for helping load broken-down or damaged vehicles.

2,143 examples of this truck tractor were delivered, 1,533 units in 1942, 130 in 1943, and 480 in 1944. The Federal Motor Truck Company, the designer of the model itself, made 1,443, the other 700 were assembled in 1942 by Reo Motors Inc., with the designation 28XS. There was practically no difference between the two if not for the little Federal fanion on the top of the radiator grille and a difference in the ventilation gills.

The UK was the foremost user of this type of trailer tractor, in the context of the Defense Aid and Lend-Lease programs. There were 1,274 examples delivered, the USSR received 234, and France 30.

The Shape

These Federal 604s were semitrailer tractors with the cabin behind the engine compartment with a

Above: For export to England, the forward lighting answered the local conditions. Note the stylized flag on the nose of the truck which was the Federal brand. (Private Collection)

Right: The presence of the headlights on either side of the radiator grille is one of the features of the Federals 604s which remained in the American armed forces, although this 6x4 diesel configuration was not the preferred solution on the other side of the Atlantic. (Private Collection)

fifth wheel at the rear. Based on a chassis with two main longerons and four principal crossmembers, this outfit had three differentials with a wheelbase of 167 inches (424.18 cm). Built with a hardtop cabin, the tractor was 97 inches high (246.38 cm). It was 95¼ inches (241.81 cm) wide and 265 inches (673.1 cm) long. It weighed in all 19,900 lb (9,035 kg); the 604 could tow semitrailers with a maximum weight

1. Windshield wiper control valve
2. Roof ventilator
3. Roof ventilator control button
4. Windshield wiper
5. Windshield quadrant
6. Windshield wiper
7. Windshield quadrant adjusting screw
8. Windshield quadrant
9. Gear shift lever
10. Auxiliary transmission lever
11. Clutch pedal
12. Brake pedal
13. Accelerator lever
14. Emergency brake lever
15. Adjustable seat cushion
16. Steering wheel
17. Cab door
18. Brake hand control valve

Extracted from the 28XS Reo manual, this shot of the driving seat gives a good idea of how a civilian cabin was militarized. (TM 10-1507)

Below: As with the Diamond T M20, the exhaust pipe exit was through the rear crossmember of the chassis; the winch was also fitted above the chassis behind the cabin. Aberdeen Proving Ground, June 5, 1942. (U.S. Army ORD-64926)

Bottom: A break for the crew of this 20-ton Truck Tractor. As often, the exhaust pipe has been modified so it could be mounted vertically on the back of the cabin. (Private Collection)

of 57,000 lb (25,878 kg) on the road but could not carry more than 19,000 lb (8,626 kg) on the tractor's fifth wheel. The braking system was of the hydraulic-vacuum type, the towed trailers having an identical braking system.

The Mechanics

Using 10.00x20 12-ply tires, the Federal rested on a free running front differential of the I-Beam-type, a 26450-W-X-3 Timken-Detroit and on two ensembles also made by Timken-Detroit, the SD-353-W-X-12. The vehicle was powered by an HB-600 Cummins diesel engine in a single block housing six pistons. This ensemble had a capacity of 672 cubic inches (11,015 cc), rated at 130.5 bhp at 2,000 rpm. It was water cooled by a radiator made up of vaned tubes and a water pump located on the front of the engine block; ventilation was by means of a six-bladed fan to increase the cooling of its 41 quarts (38.79 liters) which constituted the cooling circuit.

Top: On the banks of the River Kalapanzin in India, an unidentified British unit has just launched a barge. The carrier vehicle is one of the 1,174 Federal 604 trucks supplied under Lend-Lease to the UK. December 1944. (U.S. Army SC-348112)

Middle: At the end of its military career, this 20-ton Truck Tractor waits among other surplus vehicles to be sold to a new civilian owner who would give it a quieter civilian life. Fort Meade, May 28, 1946. (Private Collection)

Bottom: At the end of the assembly line at Reo, these 28XS intended for export have the front lighting typical of British trucks. The ventilation gills of the hood and the absence of the little fanion on the top of the radiator are specific to this builder. (Reo)

Above left: Just delivered as part of the Lend-Lease, this Federal 604 is waiting to be put into service and receive its final accessories like the spare wheel. There were 1,274 examples delivered to the UK, shared out between the various Commonwealth forces. (Federal Motor Truck Co.)

Above right: At the back of the 604's cabin, the impressive Mead Morrison-Gar Wood Model MB winch has not yet been stripped of its transport protection. (Federal Motor Truck Co.)

Below: The Australian forces were accustomed to camouflage their vehicles with 2-tone coloring. This example is coupled to a 20-ton 4-W Semitrailer of the Trailmobile type. (Federal Motor Truck Co.)

Transferring the engine drive through a single dry-disk W.C. Lippe clutch was by means of a 7881 Spicer gearbox with eight forward and two reverse gears.

With these mechanics, an 80-gallon (302.80-liter) fuel tank gave it a range of between 240 miles (384 km) unhitched and 200 miles (320 km) coupled and with a full payload, a consumption rate of between 2½ and 3 mpg; this consumption varied with the type of road, the running conditions, and the configuration—whether coupled or not.

The electrical system was very complex and worked with four 6-volt batteries grouped together two by two. Although the base current was 6 volts for most of the circuit's electrical components, the generator worked on 12 volts and the starter on 24 volts. Most of the electrical parts were made by Delco-Remy.

9 Special Series

Road Trucks

This category of road trucks concerned vehicles intended for driving along the country's roads transporting items which could be qualified as confidential and strategic.

10-Ton 6x4 E&L Transport Fleet Truck

Of all the truck tractors, the 10-ton 6x4 E&L Transport Fleet trucks were certainly the most mysterious where the mechanics, the administration, and performance were concerned. 100 were ordered with registration numbers ranging from USA-W-0101357 to USA-W-0101456. It was strange but instead of them bearing their own registration number, they bore that of the trailer which was assigned to them. This was because of a bulk order, truck and trailer, for transporting parts of heavy bombers like the Consolidated B-24 Liberator. The firm E&L Transport Company of Dearborn built the tractor and the company Handling Systems (Trailers) of Detroit the trailer.

The job was simple with two truck/trailer ensembles, one for the fuselage and the other the wings; it was a matter of convoying the parts of the plane from the factories to the assembly sites at Tulsa, Oklahoma and at Forth Worth, Texas, return trips of some 1,800 and 2,300 miles (2,900 and 3,700 km) respectively. Two Ford V8 Mercury engine blocks rated at 100 bhp, with synchronized transmissions were connected to the two rear differentials of the truck. Choosing the Ford powerplant was important as a whole logistics plan surrounded these long journeys across the United States.

In case of breakdowns, the brand's retailers situated along the way could be drawn upon. There was no military rigor in the overall design of the tractor, and several types of bodywork were used

Below: USA-W-0101416 for the 60th vehicle bought; this one has a square cab and the trailer's cutouts are very particular. (U.S. Army Signal Corps)

Bottom: At almost 72 feet (almost 22 m) long, the E&L Transport Fleet unit is a nice tractor-trailer ensemble. With USA-W-0101361 as its registration number, it is the fifth of the series with a conventional cabin. (U.S. Army Signal Corps)

Top: As well as the registration number, each tractor had several identifications, like here the 7 which was in accordance with the arithmetic group of the registration numbers. (U.S. Army Signal Corps)

Middle: Another cabin model of the sleeper-cab type with an independent sleeping cell. (U.S. Army Signal Corps)

Bottom: On September 6, 1943, a column of E&L truck tractors, stationed in Washington D.C., during an exhibition. Nobody could ignore the Ford (which built the B-24) logo on the trailers, but no mention of the trucks and the semitrailers was made. (ACME ref. W10981)

for the cabin, the availability of the parts depending on the stocks and civilian production.

This disparity was also to be noted when manufacturing the trailers; on some of them the front wheel arches were rounder and on others they were angular. Most of them were given a canvas roof whereas others consisted of rigid, sliding panels. Each tractor-trailer pair was 871 inches (2,212.34 cm) long, 106 inches (269.24 cm) wide, and 150 inches (381 cm) high, or the dimensions of a special convoy.

8-Ton 6x4 Corbitt 40SD6

Another very particular truck tractor was the Corbitt 40SD6 in its 8-ton 6x4 version. Only 44 examples were ordered with registration numbers ranging from USA-W-53771 to USA-W-53814, all delivered in 1942. Their job was like that of the E&Ls, driving along the country's roads coupled to heavy trailers transporting items that could not be handled by civilian companies.

These Corbitt 40SD-s were traditional tractors: the driving cabin was behind the engine compartment and the technical part with the fifth wheel at the rear. This ensemble had three differentials with a wheelbase of 181 inches (459.74 cm). Built with only a hardtop cabin called the sleeper cabin, the vehicle was 104 inches high (264.16 cm). It was 86 inches (218.44 cm) wide and 285 inches (723.9 cm) long.

Weighing in all 14,300 lb (6,492 kg), the 40SD6 could tow semitrailers with a maximum road weight of 50,000 lb (22,700 kg) but not carry more than 16,000 lb (7,264 kg) on the tractor's fifth wheel.

The vehicle was powered by a Continental 22R gasoline engine in a single block housing six pistons. This ensemble had a capacity of 501 cubic inches (8,212 cc), rated at 148 bhp at 2,400 rpm.

8-Ton 6x4 ACW-853 GMC

Another Truck Tractor in this very special category: the GMC ACW-853 in its 8-ton 6x6 version. Only 11 examples were ordered with registration numbers included within USA-W-51427 to USA-W-51433 and USA-W-52422 to USA-W-52425. They were all delivered in 1941. Their job was identical to that of the 40SD6.

These ACW-853s were conventional semitrailer tractors, with the driving cabin behind the engine compartment and the technical part with the fifth wheel at the rear.

This outfit had three differentials with a wheelbase of 181 inches (459.74 cm). Built only with a hardtop cabin, the vehicle was 83 inches high (210.82 cm). It was 88 inches (223.52 cm) wide and 283 inches (718.82 cm) long. It weighed in all 14,300 lb (6,492 kg). The ACW could tow semitrailers with a maximum weight of 45,000 lb (20,430 kg) but not carry more than 15,000 lb (6,810 kg) on the tractor's fifth wheel. The vehicle was powered by a GM Model 477 gasoline engine in a single block housing six pistons. This ensemble had a capacity of 477.13 cubic inches (7,820 cc), rated at 154 bhp at 2,600 rpm.

Above and left: With its fluid lines and its sleeper cab, the Corbitt 40SD6 was really a modern style vehicle. Apart from its fender hooks and its registration number, there was nothing to distinguish it from the civilian models. (Corbitt Co.)

Below left: The rare GMCs from the ACW range all had this configuration and this cabin shape which recalled that which equipped the ACKWX-353, the forerunner of the CCKWXs and CCKXs. (Private Collection)

Below right: There was no difference between the civilian and military versions. As this one has lost its fenders it's impossible to identify it by its breakdown hooks. This example is towing an FFLT Fruehauf trailer. (Private Collection)

Limited Productions

These limited series concerned vehicles intended for the Engineers, as well as those produced for the United Kingdom.

6-Ton 6x6 White 666

Accustomed to vehicles in the 6-ton category, of which the most representative is without any doubt the Brockway Bridge Construction, the Corps of Engineers received a limited series of truck tractors. They were intended to tow semitrailers

Above: A White 666 Tractor Truck being evaluated at the Desert Training Center. The first hitched up to a 20-ton Semitrailer has been loaded with a cement block; the second by itself but with a cement block as ballast, is there to push. (U.S. Army Signal Corps)

transporting the heavy equipment, for instance the D-7 or D-8 Bulldozers.

Delivered in March 1945, they only had a very limited impact on operations.

These White 666s were semitrailer tractors with the driving compartment behind the engine compartment and a technical part with a fifth wheel at the rear. This outfit had three differentials with a wheelbase of 185 inches (469.9 cm). Built with a hard- or soft-top cabin, the tractor was 110 inches high (279.4 cm) but the soft-top version enabled it to gain some 19 inches (about 50 cm) when transported by sea. It was 94½ inches (240.03 cm) wide and 285 inches (723.9 cm) long. It weighed in all 18,500 lb (8,399 kg). The White 666 could tow semitrailers with a maximum weight of 70,000 lb (31,780 kg) but not carry more than 25,000 lb (11,350 kg) on the tractor's fifth wheel. The vehicle was powered by a HXD Hercules gasoline engine in a single block housing six pistons. This engine had a capacity of 855 cubic inches (14,014 cc), rated at 202 bhp at 2,150 rpm.

Using both types of cabin for the vehicles delivered belatedly was due certainly to bodywork components being available; it was the same for the powerful 15,000-lb (6,810-kg) winch; positioned behind the cabin like on the Cargo Prime Mover, it was also situated at the front in certain cases. Very much a part of the White production, the 112 truck tractors took their place in the various supply

Below: A White 666 with a 20-ton trailer with rear motorized assistance in the Arizona dunes. (U.S. Army Signal Corps)

Left: Hoppenhein, Germany. Engineers have parked their White tractors under camouflage nets. (U.S. Army Signals Service)

Below: The Mack EHT 1942 Truck Tractors were purely civilian vehicles. It was not before the following year that they were given new bodywork. (TM 10-1546)

Bottom: The Mack Company also supplied the UK with this ST-20 Semitrailer, perfectly adapted to the EHT Tractor. (IWM)

echelons. Their registration numbers were in a series of 2,343 vehicles whose registration numbers ranged from USA-5114573 to USA-5117027.

4x2 and 4x4 Truck Tractors for the United Kingdom

In 1940, the British Army lacked equipment and more especially semitrailer tractors. As it did for many sectors, it called upon the U.S. and their Defense Aid program to be supplied rapidly. As well as the Studebaker US6 6x4 from the 2½-ton range and the Federal 20 ton, it filled the interwar period with small numbers of vehicles classified in the 5-ton category.

The Mack Company supplied 5-ton 4x2 Truck Tractors from its EH range, with 196 conventional EHT tractors including 53 for the Army (USA-544345 to USA-544397). Resting on a wheelbase of 146 inches (370.84 cm), they were powered by an EN354 Mack engine with a capacity of 354 cubic inches (5,802 cc), rated at 110 bhp at 2,620 rpm. 180 examples of the EHUT variant were built with a forward cabin. Resting on a wheelbase of 162 inches (411.48 cm), it was powered by an EN310 Mack engine with a capacity of 310 cubic inches (5,081 cc) rated at 98 bhp at 2,400 rpm.

Even more anecdotal was the firm Four Wheel Drive (FWD) which delivered 50 examples, 32 in 1942 and 18 in 1943 of its HAR-3 tractor, a conventional 4x4 5/6-ton tractor. Resting on a wheelbase of 136 inches (345.44 cm), it was powered by a BZ320 Waukesha engine with a capacity of 325 cubic inches (5,327 cc) rated at 95 bhp at 2,400 rpm.

The militarized version of the Mack EHT was principally intended for the U.S. Army. It was 216½ inches (5.5 m) long, 90½ inches (2.30 m) wide, and 86½ inches (2.20 m) high with a soft top. (Mack Corp.)

The HAR-3 from Four Wheel Drive had all the features of a civilian vehicle; it was 208 inches (5.30 m) long, 84 inches (2.15 m) wide, and 94½ inches (2.40 m) high. (FWD)

Mack's EHUT with its forward cabin was 263¾ inches (6.70 m) long, 82½ inches (2.10 m) wide and, with a soft top, 118 inches (3 m) high. (TM 10-1546)

Individual Productions

Although the different truck tractors were produced in series, prototype vehicles also existed which were not naturally associated with semitrailer tractors.

Left and below: It is difficult to imagine the Jeep Willys MT-Tug 6x6 in its tractor version. It was, however, a role to which it had been assigned ever since it was designed. 15 examples were built with in their nomenclature, the letters "TUG." The specificity being that it was able to install a fifth wheel in the rear cargo part of the vehicle; the study foresaw cargo trailers, or swan's neck vans to go over the rear of the vehicle. One single example, called T-14 Tractor and registered USA-829893, was built in this form. (U.S. Army SC-262251)

Left: The Mack NQ was a 6x6 in the 7½-ton category—the U.S. Army only ordered three examples for towing elements of 240-mm artillery pieces. While its outline suggested Mack NO, its mechanics were something else. One only remained in the form of a Heavy Tractor F-15, the two others given a cargo platform. (U.S. Army ORD-57290)

Above: The Air Force made several attempts to find the vehicle best adapted to the breakdown and recovery for aircraft on its bases. The firm Oshkosh built this sole example of the 5-ton 4x4 Truck Tractor based on its Model W709. Here in New Caledonia it has just recovered a Lockheed P-38 Lightning, November 27, 1942. (U.S. Army SC-168827)

Middle: Certainly the most extravagant of the truck tractors, this sole variant based on the Mack NO has a lengthened chassis so a crane, winch, and fifth wheel could be installed; it was given the definition Mack NO-4. This truck was assessed for the Air Forces but was not followed up. (U.S. Army Signal Corps)

Bottom: International Harvester supplied 220 examples of its KR-8 to an unidentified allied nation. This semitrailer tractor equipped with a fifth wheel and a winch behind the cabin was ordered in its 2½-ton 4x2 version. (SNL G-542)

10 Special Semitrailers

These buses, adapted from semitrailers, were a uniquely American speciality. The Army used two principal models.

6-Ton 4-Wheel 50-Passenger Semitrailer Bus

For mass movement of personnel, the Army adopted a transport method widely used in the civilian world: semitrailers designed as buses. These were basic productions for short trips on the big Army and Navy bases. For this simple job, the Ordnance Department did not wish to launch a specifically military production; it recovered the rapidly available stocks on the civilian market and dozens of companies were contacted.

The specification was simple: supply semitrailers with two axles and bodywork to transport 50 people, each trailer having to be delivered with a towing vehicle of the 1½-ton 4x2 type. The type was not important but the firms which the Army was accustomed to—Dodge, GMC, Chevrolet, etc.—were the ones chosen. The Army quickly realized that there were not enough of these trailers and so car transport semitrailers were converted. The militarization was reduced to a minimum and the tractor-trailer ensembles were painted olive drab only, the trucks being given a registration number beginning with a 3 for this tonnage category and the semitrailers beginning with the usual 0.

From this supply disparity was born a mix of trailers with quite different technical features. For example, three types of braking circuits: air, vacuum, and electrical were used, or tires with different dimensions between 7.00x20 and 8.25x20.

Thirty-one companies supplied the 1,231 50-Passenger Semitrailers to the Army. These deliveries were spread out over three years—100 units in 1942, 1,062 in 1943, and the last 69 in 1944.

1,492 truck tractors of all makes accompanied the semitrailers with 391 units in 1942, 948 in 1943, and the last 153 in 1944. But what was surprising,

Below: A typical example of the ensemble Truck Tractor–50-Passenger Semitrailer. The registration number of the GMC tractor, USA-3258742, puts it as part of production order No. T-4630 which meant it was built along with 14 other similar ensembles by the company Smith-Neil. (U.S. Army Signal Corps)

Bottom: Several differences were inevitably seen on the trailers from 31 different manufacturers. This one is coupled to a 1½-ton 4x4 G-7113-NK Chevrolet Tractor. (U.S. Army)

Top: The U.S. Navy also used the 50-Passenger Semitrailer; this example is coupled to a Chevrolet 1½-ton 4x4 tractor. The USS *Clark* (LSV-2) has just docked, coming from Guam in the Mariannas with 970 recently freed prisoners of war, September 13, 1945. (U.S. Navy)

Above: Taken from TM 9-2800, this shot gives a good impression on the 32-Passenger Semitrailer and its canvas covering.

apart from the number of trucks delivered, was their condition: 523 were secondhand having already been civilian units. When these were unavailable or broke down, they were automatically replaced by standard Truck Tractors.

2-Wheel 3-Ton 32-Passenger Bus Semitrailer

335 examples of this trailer with an outline that resembled the 6-ton Combination Animal & Cargo semitrailer were delivered in 1944 to carry horses. Once again, this was a conversion of existing materiel, a radar semitrailer from the Signal Corps. Indeed, the SCR-547 Optical Height Finder Radar was not an exceptional success and was quickly abandoned. Of the 373 operational examples, only 38 were in service, leaving 335 K-67 Antenna Mount Semitrailers available for some other use.

Everything concerned with the radar was removed from the semitrailers and they were given a wooden structure surmounted with hoops covered with special canvas and flexible windows. Four companies were entrusted with these transformations: Elizabeth City Shipyards for 110 of them, Keystone for 53, Morris Soffe for 53, and York-Hoover for the remaining 119. Deliveries were late: 294 at the end of 1944 and 41 at the beginning of 1945.

These buses with a single axle and twin 7.50x20 8-ply tires had a wheelbase of 205 inches (520.7 cm) from the axle to the coupling point for a total length of 252¼ inches (640.72 cm), a width of 96¾ inches (245.75 cm), and a tarpaulined height of 116 inches (294.64 cm). With an empty weight of 6,797 lb (3083 kg), they could take a load of 6,486 lb (2,942 kg). The distribution of the mass had 6,486 lb (2,942 kg) on its fifth wheel and 6,797 lb (3,083 kg) on the axle, a distribution ratio of 49% and 51%.

50-Passenger Semitrailer Production					
Angel Steel Stool	20	Leonhardt Wagon	33	Paramount Diners	59
Baker Trailer	79	Maday Body	96	Proctor-Keefe	16
Bartlett Trailer	10	Meyer Body	25	Schult Trailer	40
Beaver Metropolitan	150	Monpelier	25	Smith-Neil	17
Boyer Mfg.	9	Morris Soffe & Son	10	Square Deal	73
John H. Carl	42	Ohio Body	25	Swift Body	32
Fassnacht & Sons	16	Charles Olson	30	Trailer Bus Sale	23
Fitz John Coach	62	Omaha Standard	24	Twin City	32
Hackney Bros	32	Kalamazoo R.R. Supply	27	Watkins Body	73
Hess & Eisenhardt	29	Michigan Body	24		
Lacey Body	45	National Body	53	**Total**	**1,231**

Signal Corps Semitrailers

To move some of its radar and radio equipment, the Signal Corps used four models of special semitrailers.

K-67 2-Wheel 6-Ton Antenna Mount Semitrailer

Built by the Fruehauf Trailer Co. and called the K-67, out of the 373 examples ordered, only 38 were operational; the other 335 were transformed into 32-passenger buses.

Built on a profiled chassis resting on a single axle, it was fitted with two sets of twinned wheels 7.50x60, 8-ply with two jockey wheels and two folding stabilizers. Its tractor was the 1½-ton 4x4 Chevrolet Truck Tractor which was so equipped to ensure that its electric braking system worked.

These semitrailers had a 205-inch (520.7-cm) wheelbase—axle to coupling point—for a total length 252¼ inches (640.72 cm), a width of 96¾ inches (245.75 cm), and a height of 120 inches (304.8 cm) with the antenna folded. With a full payload it weighed 11,503 lb (5,218 kg). The distribution of the mass had 6,505 lb (2,951 kg) on its fifth wheel and 4,998 lb (2,267 kg) on its axle, a distribution ratio of 56% and 44%.

Above: Halelwa, Oahu Island, Hawaii, an SCR-547 Optical Height Finder Radar is in surveillance position, in tandem with an SCR-268 Mobile Long Wave Searchlight Control Set, visible behind it. An M1 Rangefinder adds to the accuracy of the work of the teams watching the electronics. (U.S. Army Air Forces ref 65278 A.C.)

Above left: Factory-new and without the radar components installed, the K-67 semitrailer is simply an offset flatbed. (TM 9-2 800)

Left: The K-22 semitrailer was a complete outfit including the chassis, the axle, the turntable, and the jib boom. Setting it all up was by sliding the tower forward then adjusting it, a maneuver carried out with the help of the two winches equipping the outfit. (TM-2800)

K-22 2-Wheel 8-Ton Antenna Mount Semitrailer

This semitrailer took the immense antenna of the SCR-270 radar. Creating it was the collaboration between the firms Kingham Trailer Co. for the chassis and Couse Laboratories for the antenna mast. Called K-22 for the first ones delivered, they subsequently became the K-64 or K-71. The three appellations applied to the same trailer.

They differed only in minor details, like the electric powering of the winch used to mount the antenna or that used to rotate the ensemble, or even redesigning the mast pivoting and lifting system. 158 trailers of this type were manufactured.

This very secret material was made up of a semitrailer-type chassis mounted on a fixed axle with two twinned wheels, a mast, like those of drilling rigs, which was folded or lifted by activating two winches, and a base pivoting through 360°. Once deployed, the aerial was 55 feet (16.78 m) high with an 8-foot (2.44-m) base and it was on this that the panels were fixed to form the antenna. These semitrailers with a single axle and twinned 7.50x20 8-ply wheels had a 260-inch (660.4-cm) wheelbase—axle to coupling point—for a total length of 363 inches (922.02 cm), a width of 95¼ inches (241.93 cm), and a height of 123 inches (312.42 cm) with the antenna folded. With a full payload, it weighed 15,712 lb (7,127 kg) and needed a tractor in the 4/5-ton category to move it and get its compressed-air braking system working.

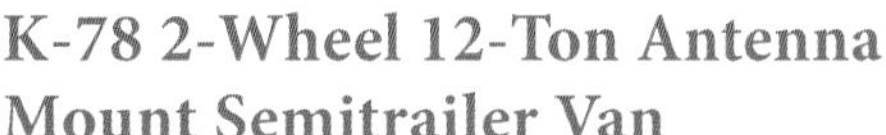

K-78 2-Wheel 12-Ton Antenna Mount Semitrailer Van

Designated as the K-78 by the Signal Corps, this semitrailer van was designed to contain all the controlling elements of the SCR-584 Anti-Aircraft Fire Control radar and support its aerial. It was traditionally manufactured with a side access and rear modulable panels. Mounted on an axle with twin wheels, it did not matter which tractor in the 4/5-ton category it used to move it and to get its compressed-air braking system to work.

These semitrailers had a 192-inch (488.32-cm) wheelbase, axle to coupling point. It was 245½ inches (623.57 cm) long, 97¼ inches (247.02 cm) wide, and 125¼ inches (318.14 cm) high without the radar antenna. Weighing with a full payload 18,541 lb (8,410 kg), the weight was distributed with 6,907 lb (3,133 kg) resting on the tractor's fifth wheel and 11,633 lb (5,277 kg) on its axle, a weight distribution ratio of 37% to 63%. 150 examples of these trailers with a single axle and twinned 9.00x20 10-ply tires were made by Fruehauf, each having a specific dolly, which the Signal Corps called K-83.

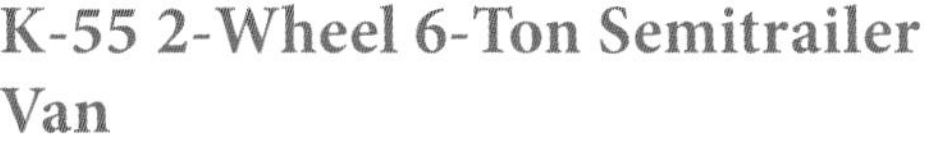

K-55 2-Wheel 6-Ton Semitrailer Van

A large-sized semitrailer, the K-55 can be considered as a general-purpose trailer, able to take radio equipment as well as being used as a meeting room or a mobile HQ.

Above: The SCR-270 Warning Radar worked throughout the Second World War; this example is in position on Okinawa in 1945. Despite its impressive dimensions, including its almost 669 inches (17 m) height, its light structure made it difficult to see. (U.S. Army Air Forces ref. 39746 A.C.)

Left: Oahu, October 9, 1945, at the 584th Signal Depot Repair Shop. Two new SCR-584s have just been unloaded; their trailers are still caulked for sea transport, at the door and panel joints. The two semitrailers have been assembled with K-83 dollies. (U.S. Army SC-218251)

Built by the companies A.J. Miller and Oneonta Linn., the K-55s were vans placed on a chassis resting on two single-wheeled axles of the 7.50x30 8-ply type. The integral bodywork was fitted with two large doors at the rear, a small side access door and various closable windows; it had the advantage of offering a volume of transport greater than the trucks in the van niche. Various versions classified from B to E succeeded each other all throughout production with the particularity of using an electric braking system, which was consistent with its tractor, the 1½-ton 4x4 Chevrolet. There were 98 examples delivered, USA-0102824 to USA-0102916 and USA-090808 to USA-090813.

These vans with a double axle and 7.50 8-ply wheels have a 215-inch (546.1-cm) wheelbase, axle to coupling point). It was 312¼ inches (793.12 cm) long, 96 inches (243.84 cm) wide, and 117¾ inches (299.09 cm) high. Weighing 8,587 lb (3,895 kg) empty, it could take a weight of 3,503 lb (1,589 kg). With a full payload, the weight was distributed with 5,606 lb (2,543 kg) resting on the tractor's fifth wheel and 6,484 lb (2,941 kg) on its axle, a weight distribution ratio of 46% to 54%.

Top: Installing an SCR-594 Anti-Aircraft Fire Control Set in the Philippines in 1945. Not counting digging the protective trench, it only took half an hour to install this type of radar, compared with six hours for the old SCR-268. (U.S. Army Air Forces ref. 60720 A.C.)

Middle: A K-55 Semitrailer set up. This example houses an SCR-698. Space was so important that it was possible to install the apparatuses and still leave space for maintenance and component repairs. (Signal Corps SCL-5865)

Below: April 1942, Fort Monmouth. The presentation of a K-73 Chevrolet Truck Tractor and K-55 Semitrailer. The trailer's dimensions are impressive and provide a large, covered workspace for the operators. (U.S. Army SC-133821)

Dollies

These special accessories transformed a semitrailer into a normal trailer so that it could be coupled to a standard truck or become part of a transport train.

A semitrailer without a tractor was a dead weight. Equipping it with a dolly transformed the semitrailer into a traditional trailer which could be moved by a normal tractor or any other handling vehicle. It became interesting in the depots when loads were prepared or during moves when driving conditions permitted several semitrailers to be towed by the same tractor. It is complicated to compile a list of the many types of dollies bought by the American armed forces.

Left: The very first dollies for C-2 Semitrailers were supplied in 1939 by the firm Corbitt at the same time as the truck tractors and their trailers. (U.S. Army Signal Corps)

Below: On the deck of a transport ship, these two F2 2,000-gallon Semitankers are mounted on their specific dollies. Although not always listed, they each have a special registration number beginning with a zero like the trailers. (U.S. Army SC-168450)

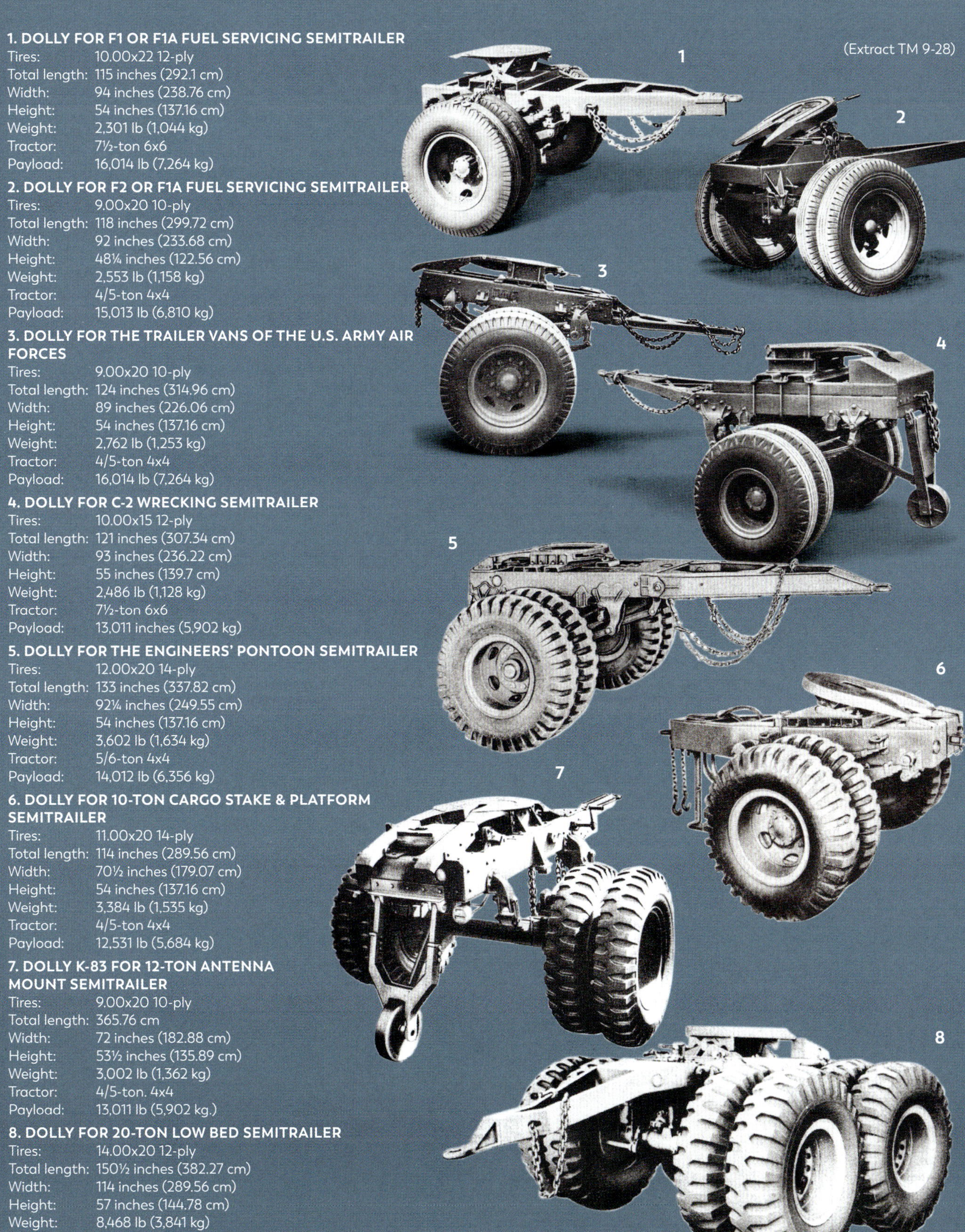

1. DOLLY FOR F1 OR F1A FUEL SERVICING SEMITRAILER
Tires: 10.00x22 12-ply
Total length: 115 inches (292.1 cm)
Width: 94 inches (238.76 cm)
Height: 54 inches (137.16 cm)
Weight: 2,301 lb (1,044 kg)
Tractor: 7½-ton 6x6
Payload: 16,014 lb (7,264 kg)

2. DOLLY FOR F2 OR F1A FUEL SERVICING SEMITRAILER
Tires: 9.00x20 10-ply
Total length: 118 inches (299.72 cm)
Width: 92 inches (233.68 cm)
Height: 48¼ inches (122.56 cm)
Weight: 2,553 lb (1,158 kg)
Tractor: 4/5-ton 4x4
Payload: 15,013 lb (6,810 kg)

3. DOLLY FOR THE TRAILER VANS OF THE U.S. ARMY AIR FORCES
Tires: 9.00x20 10-ply
Total length: 124 inches (314.96 cm)
Width: 89 inches (226.06 cm)
Height: 54 inches (137.16 cm)
Weight: 2,762 lb (1,253 kg)
Tractor: 4/5-ton 4x4
Payload: 16,014 lb (7,264 kg)

4. DOLLY FOR C-2 WRECKING SEMITRAILER
Tires: 10.00x15 12-ply
Total length: 121 inches (307.34 cm)
Width: 93 inches (236.22 cm)
Height: 55 inches (139.7 cm)
Weight: 2,486 lb (1,128 kg)
Tractor: 7½-ton 6x6
Payload: 13,011 inches (5,902 kg)

5. DOLLY FOR THE ENGINEERS' PONTOON SEMITRAILER
Tires: 12.00x20 14-ply
Total length: 133 inches (337.82 cm)
Width: 92¼ inches (249.55 cm)
Height: 54 inches (137.16 cm)
Weight: 3,602 lb (1,634 kg)
Tractor: 5/6-ton 4x4
Payload: 14,012 lb (6,356 kg)

6. DOLLY FOR 10-TON CARGO STAKE & PLATFORM SEMITRAILER
Tires: 11.00x20 14-ply
Total length: 114 inches (289.56 cm)
Width: 70½ inches (179.07 cm)
Height: 54 inches (137.16 cm)
Weight: 3,384 lb (1,535 kg)
Tractor: 4/5-ton 4x4
Payload: 12,531 lb (5,684 kg)

7. DOLLY K-83 FOR 12-TON ANTENNA MOUNT SEMITRAILER
Tires: 9.00x20 10-ply
Total length: 365.76 cm
Width: 72 inches (182.88 cm)
Height: 53½ inches (135.89 cm)
Weight: 3,002 lb (1,362 kg)
Tractor: 4/5-ton. 4x4
Payload: 13,011 lb (5,902 kg.)

8. DOLLY FOR 20-TON LOW BED SEMITRAILER
Tires: 14.00x20 12-ply
Total length: 150½ inches (382.27 cm)
Width: 114 inches (289.56 cm)
Height: 57 inches (144.78 cm)
Weight: 8,468 lb (3,841 kg)
Tractor: of various sizes
Payload: 16,014 lb (7,264 kg)

The Engineers had dollies mainly for their fuel tankers and their pontoon trailers and the Air Forces for their C-2 Semitrailers as well as their Fuel Tankers and Field Shops. But there was no standardization to obtain the same series, each supplier delivering its own model simply adapted to its military recommendations.

As for the signals, 400 dollies were listed for the K-67 Antenna Mount Semitrailers, 150 for the K-78 Antenna Mount Semitrailers, and 734 for the 10-ton Stake & Platform Semitrailers.

The Ordnance Department was more structured with its purchases; in three large categories, 400 3-ton dollies were bought from Fruehauf in 1944, 2,014 6-ton dollies were supplied by the Heil Company spread out between 1943 and 1945, and 1,000 10-ton dollies were ordered from the Production Engineer Company together with another 2,000 examples from the Springfield Auto Works.

Above: The dolly seen here highlights its importance, enabling the semitrailer to be handled without it having to use its dedicated tractor. The semitrailer is landed on the quayside and taken in hand by a handling vehicle. (U.S. Army SC-170960)

Below: On Okinawa, in the Ryukyus Archipelago, a Field Repair Shop Semitrailer for flight instruments rests on its dolly whose tires have been protected from the sun. (U.S. Army Air Forces ref. 63883 A.C.)

Postwar

The end of hostilities did not mean the end of a career for most truck tractors.

With May 8, 1945 over, the enormous amount of materiel used to defeat Germany became a huge logistics problem and, above all, a financial headache for America. Huge numbers of these surplus vehicles were sold on the spot, both to civilians as well as to Allied armies. Generally, all these vehicles were delivered as they were, be the condition good, bad, or average. Some countries, like France, organized workovers after dismantling them totally. At Neuvy-Pailloux, Indre, thousands of American vehicles underwent a total facelift.

In the United States, large auction sales of used vehicles were organized. The Army also renewed its cartage by putting into service the last vehicles

The Red River Arsenal, Texas, July 14, 1950. Hundreds of truck tractors are assembled there before mothballing. After this long-term storage, they were all upgraded. (U.S. Army SC-342219)

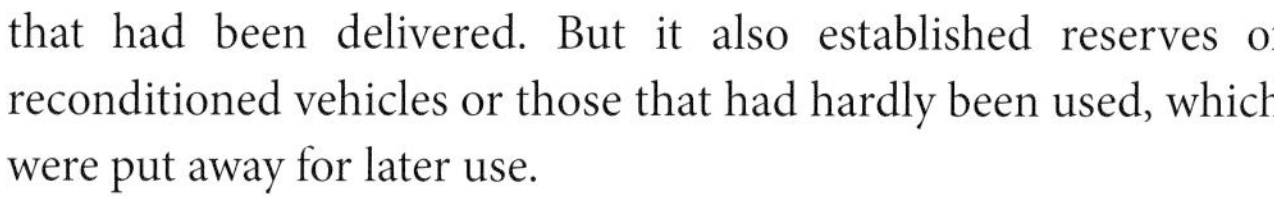

that had been delivered. But it also established reserves of reconditioned vehicles or those that had hardly been used, which were put away for later use.

This way of getting rid of or freezing an enormous number of vehicles enabled new materiel to be developed and new orders to be made for industry to support the economy.

In Europe, particularly in Germany, a vast program for reconditioning wheeled vehicles was established. Industrial installations were requisitioned and assigned to get the vehicle park back up to normal levels. Each depot specialized in certain categories of vehicles. For example, the Aalen Ordnance Maintenance Depot, run by the 51st Ordnance Group, worked on buses and trucks over 4 tons with a special orientation toward the truck tractors. Located at Aalen, an industrial city in Baden-Württemberg, it functioned between December 6, 1946 and early 1953 thanks to local labor, employing 1,400 civilians.

1. In the old Maschinenfabrik Alfing factory in Aalen, the vehicles arrived by rail to be reconditioned; here 5-ton International and 4/5-ton Autocar Truck Tractors.

2. Before any work was done, the vehicles were entirely cleaned with high-pressure hoses.

3. The first steps consisted of dismantling everything, starting with the removable parts of the bodywork, hood, windshield, etc.

4. All the engine systems and all the cabin accessories were carefully removed and sent to the reconditioning workshops.

5. Dismantling and storage of the cabins that were sent to the bodywork and paint workshops. They were entirely sanded before being treated with an anticorrosive product, a new olive drab livery, and the regulation markings.

6. In the workshop, all the parts were removed from the chassis and entirely reviewed and reconditioned. The seals, ball bearings, crosspieces, and all the components likely to wear were replaced.

7. and 8. Dismantling continued, as each subgroup was inspected and refurbished, the last step consisting of stripping down to a bare chassis before proceeding with a complete rebuild. It was shown that this solution of doing the work in Germany was way cheaper than going home for the same operation with the original manufacturers and/or purchasing new vehicles.

9. Entirely reconditioned from a mechanical point of view, with new tires and new paintwork, these International Harvester M-426s are waiting to return to the depots. A postwar particularity, the registration number has lost its S which defined the vehicles given interference suppression for radio installations. (Private Collection)

Appendix

Total Production

Covering the period 1939–45, production of standard truck tractors represents 68,756 trucks shared among 18 large manufacturers who supplied 37 different models in 10 or so weight categories.

Truck Tractors				
Manufacturers	Models	Category	Mount	Production
Autocar Company	U-4044	2½-ton	4x4	548 examples
	U-4144-T	2½-ton	4x4	271 examples
	U-7144-T	4/5-ton	4x4	11,104 examples
	U-5044	5-ton	4x4	97 examples
	U-8144-T	5/6-ton	4x4	2,711 examples
	U-8244-T	5/6-ton	4x4	90 examples
Biederman Motors Corporation	Fuel Servicing Type F1	7½-ton	6x6	953 examples
	Wrecking Type C-2	7½-ton	6x6	10 examples
Chevrolet Motor Division GMC	WA & G-4103	1½-ton	4x2	891 examples
	G-4112 4165 7113	1½-ton	4x4	2,943 examples
Corbitt Company	40SD6	8-ton	6x4	44 examples
	Wrecking Type C-2	7½-ton	6x6	4 examples
	Fuel Servicing Type F1	7½-ton	6x6	17 examples
Dodge Brothers Corporation	T-118	1½-ton	4x2	116 examples
E&L Transport Company	–	10-ton	6x4	100 examples
Federal Motor Truck Company	94x43 (A B & C)	4/5-ton	4x4	8,119 examples
	Model 604	20-ton	6x4	1,443 examples
	Wrecking Type C-2	7½-ton	6x6	2,667 examples
	Fuel Servicing Type F1	7½-ton	6x6	200 examples
Ford Motor Co.	2GT & 2GT8	1½-ton	4x2	1,114 examples
Four Wheel Drive	HAR-3	5/6-ton	4x4	50 examples
GMC Truck & Coach	AFKX-502	2½-ton	4x4	81 examples
	ACW-853	8-ton	6x4	11 examples
International Harvester Company	KR-11	5-ton	4x2	1,232 examples
	H-542-9 / M-425	5-ton	4x2	4,640 examples
	H-542-11 / M-426	5-ton	4x2	6,678 examples
	KR-8	2½-ton	4x2	220 examples
Kenworth Motor Truck Corporation	H-542-11 / M-426	5-ton	4x2	1,100 examples
Mack Manufacturing Corp.	EHT	5-ton	4x2	196 examples
	EHUT	5-ton	4x2	180 examples
	NJU-1/2	5/6-ton	4x4	700 examples
Marmon-Herrington Company	H-542-11 / M-426	5-ton	4x2	3,200 examples
Reo Motors Inc.	Model 28XS	20-ton	6x4	700 examples
	Fuel Servicing Type F1	7½-ton	6x6	1,959 examples

Pacific Car & Foundry Company	M-26	12-ton	6x6	753 examples
	M-26A1	12-ton	6x6	619 examples
Studebaker Corporation	US6x4-U6	2½-ton	6x4	8,640 examples
White Motor Company	Model 444	4/5-ton	4x4	2,751 examples
	Model 666	6-ton	6x6	112 examples
Divers	For Bus 50 p.	1½-ton	4x2	1,492 examples
Total				**68,756 examples**

Semitrailers

Model	Category	Mount	Production
3-ton Bus 32-Passenger Semitrailer	3-ton (6-ton Gross)	2 wheels	335 examples
3½-ton Stake & Platform (S&P) Semitrailer	3½-ton (6-ton Gross)	2 wheels	1,818 examples
3½-ton Van Semitrailer	3½-ton (6-ton Gross)	2 wheels	2,259 examples
5-ton Van Refrigerator Semitrailer	5-ton (10-ton Gross)	2 wheels	239 examples
5-ton Stake & Platform (S&P) Semitrailer	5-ton (10-ton Gross)	2 wheels	8,107 examples
6-ton Bus 50-Passenger Semitrailer	6-ton (10-ton Gross)	4 wheels	1,231 examples
6-ton Combination Animal & Cargo Semitrailer	6-ton (10-ton Gross)	2 wheels	1,188 examples
6-ton Van Laundry Semitrailer	6-ton (10-ton Gross)	2 wheels	1,335 examples
6-ton Van Sterilizer & Bath Semitrailer	6-ton (10-ton Gross)	2 wheels	162 examples
6-ton Van Mobile Records Units Semitrailer	6-ton (10-ton Gross)	2 wheels	276 examples
6-ton Van Clothing Repair Semitrailer	6-ton (10-ton Gross)	2 wheels	131 examples
6-ton Van Textile Repair Semitrailer	6-ton (10-ton Gross)	2 wheels	125 examples
6-ton Van Shoe Repair Semitrailer	6-ton (10-ton Gross)	2 wheels	146 examples
Water Tank 1,500 gallons Semitrailer	6-ton (10-ton Gross)	2 wheels	± 594 examples
Gas Tank 2000 gallons (Model F2 & F2A) Semitrailer	6-ton (10-ton Gross)	2 wheels	4,032 examples
6-ton Van Semitrailer	6-ton (10-ton Gross)	2 wheels	5,248 examples
Semitrailer 6-ton Van for USAAF	6-ton (10-ton Gross)	2 wheels	898 examples
6-ton Map Reproduction Semitrailer	6-ton (10-ton Gross)	2 wheels	43 examples
7-ton Cargo (wooden superstructure version) Semitrailer	7-ton (10-ton Gross)	2 wheels	5,410 examples
7-ton Cargo (metal superstructure version) Semitrailer	7-ton (10-ton Gross)	2 wheels	1,654 examples
10-ton Stake & Platform (S&P) Semitrailer	10-ton (14-ton Gross)	2 wheels	18,938 examples
Semitrailer for 10-ton Pontoon	–	2 wheels	± 400 examples
Semitrailer for 25-ton Pontoon	–	2 wheels	± 3,500 examples
M15 Semitrailer	–	–	1,294 examples
M15A1 Semitrailer	–	–	916 examples
Wrecking C-2 25- & 40-feet Semitrailer	–	–	± 3,000 examples
Semitrailer Fuel Servicing F-1 & F-1A	–	–	± 3,000 examples
Signal Corps Antenna Mount K-67 Semitrailer	(6-ton Gross)	2 wheels	38 examples
Signal Corps Antenna Mount K-22 Semitrailer	(8-ton Gross)	2 wheels	158 examples
Signal Corps Antenna Mount K-78 Semitrailer	(12-ton Gross)	2 wheels	150 examples
Signal Corps Van K-55 Semitrailer	(6-ton Gross)	4 wheels	98 examples
Total			**66,723 examples**

The complete range of vehicles, among which 4/5-ton 4x4 Autocar and Federal Truck Tractors are all mixed up. Photographed in the Paris region, the trucks are those of the 53rd Mobile Record Unit (MRU) of the Seine Section (SS) of Company Z. (Private Collection)

Bibliography

Principal Manuals and Catalogs

SNL: Standard Nomenclature List
TB: Technical Bulletin
TM: Technical Manual
SNL G-508 General Motors 2½-ton, 6x6 Model CCKW-352/353. June 15, 1945.
SNL G-510 Autocar U-7144-U & White Model 444. June 1, 1945.
SNL G-513 Federal 4–5-ton, 4x4 Model 94x43 Truck Tractor. November 10, 1944.
SNL G-542 International Harvester 5-ton, 4x2. September 2, 1944.
SNL G-544 Semitrailer Cargo 7-ton (Service Parts Catalogue). June 20, 1944.
SNL G-545 Semitrailer Van 6-ton (Service Parts Catalogue). February 1, 1944.
SNL G-655 General Motors Master Parts List. November 1, 1943.
SNL G-659 International Harvester Master Parts Book. September 15, 1943.
SNL G-675 Semitrailer Stake and Platform 5-ton (Service Parts Catalogue). May 15, 1944.
SNL G-676 Semitrailer Stake and Platform 10-ton (Service Parts Catalogue). 1944.
SNL G-678 Semitrailer Gas 2,000-gallon (Service Parts Catalogue). November 15, 1944.
TB 5-9720-15 Technical Data for Trailers. March 1945.
TM5-270 Standard Stream Crossing Equipment. November 1, 1940.
TM5-273 25-ton Pontoon Bridge Model 1940. August 1, 1942.
TM5-9312 Semitrailer Water 1,500-gallon. February 9, 1944.
TM9-767 40-ton Tank Transporter. February 23, 1944.
TM9-801 General Motors 2½ton, 6x6 Model CCKW-352/353. April 24, 1944.
TM9-812 International Harvester 5-ton, 4x2 Model M-425 & M-426. February 15, 1944.
TM9-816 Autocar 4–5-ton, 4x4 Model U-7144-T Truck Tractor. March 21, 1944.
TM9-817 Autocar 5–6-ton, 4x4 Model U-8144-T Pontoon Truck Tractor. (TM) April 10, 1944.
TM9-820 Federal 4–5-ton, 4x4 Model 94x43 Truck Tractor. March 15, 1944.
TM9-823 International Harvester 5-ton, 4x2 Model KR-11, 1944.
TM9-882 Semitrailer Panel Cargo 7-ton. June 11, 1943.
TM9-890 Semitrailer Stake and Platform 5-ton. July 12, 1944.
TM9-892 Semitrailer Stake and Platform 10-ton. April 22, 1944.
TM9-2700 Principles of Automotive Vehicles. November 18, 1947.
TM9-2800 Military Vehicles. October 1947.
TM9-2800 Standard Military Motor Vehicles. September 1, 1943.
TM9-2800-1 Military Vehicles. September 1953.
TM10-1107 Federal 4–5-ton, 4x4 Model 94x43 Truck Tractor (Maintenance Manual). July 10, 1941.
TM10-1119 Autocar 5–6-ton, 4x4 Model U-8144-T Pontoon Truck Tractor (Maintenance Manual). February 4, 1942.
TM10-1407 Federal 4–5-ton, 4x4 Model 94x43 Truck Tractor (Maintenance Manual). 15 September 15, 1942.
TM10-1457 Federal 20-ton, 6x4 Model 604 Truck Tractor (Maintenance Manual). February 1944.
TM10-1507 Reo 20-ton, 6x4 Model 28XS Truck Tractor (Maintenance Manual). June 1943.
TM10-1546 Mack 5-ton, 4x2 Model EHT et EHUT (Maintenance Manual). August 1942.
TM10-1565 Studebaker US6 6x4 Model U6 (Maintenance Manual). September 15, 1942.
TM10-1701 General Motors 2½-ton, 4x4 Model AFKX-502 (Maintenance Manual). August 20, 1941.
TM10-1705 Mack 5–6-ton, 4x4 Model NJU-1 Pontoon Truck Tractor (Maintenance Manual). May 1941.

Documentation and Publications

Andres, Didier, *U.S. Army Chevrolet Trucks in World War II*. Casemate, 2020.
Andres, Didier. *U.S. Army Diamond T Vehicles in World War II*. Casemate, 2022.
Crismon, Fred W. *U.S. Military Wheeled Vehicles*. Crestline Publishing, 1983.
Engineering of Transport Vehicles, 1942–1945. Chief of Ordnance–Detroit, 1945.
Lend-Lease Shipments World War II. Office of the Chief of Finance, War Department, December 31, 1946.
Official Production of the United States, July 1, 1940 to August 31, 1945. May 1, 1947.
Ordnance Department, Administrative and Tactical Vehicles, 1940–1944. Automotive Center. January 1, 1944.
Ordnance Department, Administrative and Tactical Armored Vehicles, 1940–1945. Automotive Center. 1 May 1, 1945.
Ordnance Department, Administrative and Tactical Vehicles, 1940–1945. Automotive Center. October 1, 1945.
Summary Report of Acceptances, Tank-Automotive Material, 1940–1945. Chief of Ordnance–Detroit, 1945.
Vanderveen, Bart H. *The Observer's Fighting Vehicles Directory*. London: Frederick Warne & Co. Ltd., 1972.
Vanderveen, Bart H. *Wheels & Tracks: Historic Military Vehicles Directory*. London: Battle of Britain Prints International, 1989.